Women

of the

Apache

Nation

Women

VOICES OF TRUTH

of the

H. HENRIETTA STOCKEL

Apache

Foreword by Dan L. Thrapp

Nation

University of Nevada Press   Reno & Las Vegas

The paper used in this book meets the minimum requirements of American National Standard for Information Sciences—Permanence of Paper for Printed Library Materials, ANSI Z39.48-1984. Binding materials were chosen for strength and durability.

Stockel, H. Henrietta, 1938–
Women of the Apache nation : voices of truth / H. Henrietta Stockel ; foreword by Dan L. Thrapp.
p.   cm.
Includes bibliographical references and index.
ISBN 0-87417-168-7 (alk. paper)
1. Apache Indians—Women—Interviews.   2. Apache Indians—Rites and ceremonies.   3. Apache Indians—Legends.
4. Women soldiers—Southwest, New.   5. Indians of North America—South, New—Women.
E99.A6S76   1991
305.48'8972079—dc20
90–22003
CIP

University of Nevada Press,
Reno, Nevada 89557 USA
Copyright © 1991 University of Nevada Press
Designed by Richard Hendel
Printed in the United States of America
9 8 7 6 5 4 3 2 1

to . . .

the *Gah'e* who dance in my heart

and to . . .

the memory of the Chiricahua prisoners of war

with respect and reverence

The U.S. Army adopted the

figure of the "kneeling squaw"

as its target in rifle

practice.

    —Stan Steiner,

      The Waning of the West

Contents

Foreword

   Books about the Apache Indians of the Southwest number in
the hundreds. They concern the tribesmen themselves, their ethnology,
life-style, mythology, history, and, above all, their record of warfare, prin-
cipally against the whites who invaded, conquered, and eventually settled
their lands. The one aspect almost none of these volumes reflect is the
half of the Apache nations—and there are several of them—who were
coequally responsible for all of the foregoing: the women.

   It is a given that without them there would be no Apache people. But
that they had an important role in virtually every aspect of Apache life is
not so well understood. They not only assumed the domestic functions,
or most of them, but they also supported the hunters by providing them
with the food they required for their long searches for game, by which

the people largely existed, and frequently informed the men when it was time to hunt, if they wanted to eat. The women dressed the meat the men brought back, tanned the skins for a variety of purposes, and made the clothing, while also raising the corn in the tiny patches the Indians cultivated in secluded glens and brewing the tiswin that kept their men happy at intervals. Some of them, a very few, may even have accompanied raiding or war parties, and it was to the women that returning warriors often turned over any adult male prisoners they had brought back for such dire endings as made the Apaches famed and feared for generations.

With all of these indispensable roles, why have Apache women been so neglected by white investigators, save for ethnologists and collectors of such superb artifacts—created by women—as baskets, water jars, buckskin handicrafts, and other things? In the popular literature they seem always to have been passed over, and quite undeservedly so.

In the book you are holding, you will find the first major work on Apache women devoted to themselves almost exclusively. That alone should make it of intense interest. And in addition to its chosen subject matter, you will find that it also is solidly researched from primary sources, that it is intensely accurate, very readable, and honest, and, in short, is a revealing study of this much-neglected field.

It is more than that, though.

As the narration unfolds, the author's knowledge of her Apache informants becomes steadily clearer as she probes deeply into their private and wholly captivating world. The book parallels this evolution of understanding by becoming a highly personal narrative of the transformation of the writer herself from a talented inquirer delving into a foreign field, through awareness of the uniqueness of this selected area of research, into a metamorphosis so compelling that she actually becomes, in the final episode, almost an Apache woman herself.

It is thus an entrancing tale wrapped in a study of an engrossing subject now on the point of vanishing forever as the "old ones," her informants, near their own departure. Henrietta Stockel undertook this significant study just in time.

For her it was rather a long road to the project represented in these absorbing pages, or a very lengthy apprenticeship, if you will. Born in Perth

Amboy, New Jersey, about as remote from Apacheland as it is possible for a person to be and still reside in the United States, she early showed promise as a writer, publishing her first essay, she reports, when she was seven years old. Her fascination with Indians began at an early age:

> The way I became interested in Indians was through the Saturday afternoon movies when, as a child, I enjoyed all the cowboy and Indian shows. In particular, whenever the Apaches were the enemy, which was not seldom, it seemed to evoke a more intense reaction by the army officers and soldiers. Within that framework the Chiricahua Apaches and Cochise and Geronimo seemed the most fearsome. My imagination was as much a captive of the Chiricahuas as was the blonde girl child upon the silver screen whom the Apaches inevitably stole away from her happy home on a ranch. At the end of the movie, and the afternoon, the little prisoner and I always somehow found our separate ways back home, she in the kindly arms of a cavalry officer and I on the local bus. I wonder what would have happened to both of us if the Indians had won? Just once?

She acknowledges that the fascination with the Chiricahuas was at least partially responsible for her move from New York City to Santa Fe in 1974, "before the town became a trendy, fashionable place to live."

By that time she had been a technical writer and editor, a public information specialist, and, following her arrival at Santa Fe, a program administrator at Santa Fe and Albuquerque for the New Mexico State Human Services Department. Meanwhile she pursued her avocational interests as a writer of nonfiction, fiction, and poetry and had intensified her fascination with Apaches and Indian affairs to the point where she was a board member of the Albuquerque American Indian Center and had served as consultant to the Mescalero Apache Tribe on social welfare programs and "grantsmanship," a word that she may or may not have coined but is self-explanatory. She now writes nearly full time and lives pleasantly with two cats, The Marshal and Miss Kitty, both names seemingly devolved from the long-running television series *Gunsmoke*, and a Bearded Collie named Sagebrush Benedict, in Rio Rancho, a few miles upriver from Albuquerque.

Her writing is justifiably becoming widely known. She coauthored one earlier book with Bobette Perrone and Victoria Kreuger, the well-received *Medicine Women, Curanderas, and Women Doctors*. She is working hard to complete still another book, *The Medical History of the Chiricahua Apaches*, which has become, she confesses, "practically a full-time job in itself."

Henrietta Stockel reveals in her preface how she was softly rebuffed at the outset of her research into the study that resulted in *Women of the Apache Nation*. She had called a Mescalero Apache woman to ask for an interview, when the voice at the other end of the line cut in with, "Why would I want to talk to you about anything?" Stockel thought for a moment, saw the justice in the Apache's question, thanked her, and hung up. She had much to learn about Apaches before she would get anywhere with her undertaking, and she knew it.

Perhaps it was at that time that she became acquainted with the late Eve Ball, the legendary white woman of Ruidoso, New Mexico, who over a period of many years had become the trusted confidante, friend, and recorder of those Chiricahua and Warm Springs Apaches who had been brought to Mescalero from their Fort Sill exile, most of whom had reason to trust no other white person at all. At any rate, Mrs. Ball and Henrietta Stockel became friends, and from Mrs. Ball she learned a great deal about Apaches, how to deserve and win their trust and best gain their cooperation on a serious study such as hers. "Gradually," she says, "they started talking with me, and the book took shape."

As she explains in her preface, and as the reader will delightfully learn from the work itself, the book is a compilation of the skillfully assembled and excellently narrated stories of four paradigmatical Apache women. Their life patterns may differ in externals, but each embodies the indestructible qualities and mind sets of the traditional women of The People: Elbys Naiche Hugar, Kathleen Smith Kanseah, Mildred Imach Cleghorn, and Ruey Haozous Darrow. Her selection of these four seems inspired. No matter what their living patterns today, and how varied they are, each has retained and lives by the solid core of her inheritance. Each is intelligent, knowledgeable, and outspoken with this white woman who has become a friend, and to some extent confidante, and honest in what she shares with her. This speaks well for the skills, dedication, persistence, and integrity with which Henrietta Stockel has pursued her investigative crusade.

The book winds up, as it should, with her moving experience when she takes part in the dance with the *Gah'e*, or the Mountain Spirits, a traditional, emotionally moving, and spiritual event of meaningful grace, song, and movement that incorporates much of the Apache élan.

Wearing the necessary shawl through an evening almost too warm for it, she hesitantly, rather clumsily, followed Mildred Cleghorn into the dance pattern along with other Apaches but no other white person. She found the effort wearying and felt increasingly awkward and out of place. Henrietta lost the rhythm, she tired, her shoulders sagged; she tried futilely to regain the step but couldn't. Exhausted, wholly dismayed, she thought herself a failure when a male Apache's voice called to her from beyond the firelight: "That's all right, white woman! Don't worry. You're doing just fine!" She never learned who he was, but for his cheerful call "I shall be eternally grateful," she wrote.

Instantly she fell into the rhythm anew, swung her shoulders in time with Mildred Cleghorn, and followed her feet with new success. "And I prayed . . . just as the Apache women in line behind me were doing, and just as generations of Apache women have done. At long last, I felt part of the ancient, sacred ceremony. At long last, I was truly dancing with the *Gah'e*."

Finally, she *was* Apache. The triumph of her study, the conclusion of her research, the end of her pilgrimage. She had *arrived*—and the account of it all is in this remarkable book.

DAN L. THRAPP

Preface

Apache women yesterday. The words create first a vision, a swirling image of riders on horseback, long black hair streaming as they, carrying children in cradleboards on their backs, gallop behind the warriors yet well ahead of the enemy. In extreme contrast, the words also raise a picture of a peaceful camp where children play and women weave baskets and tan hides, cook, talk, and laugh together.

Apache women today. Elbys Naiche Hugar does traditional beadwork, extemporaneously sings into a microphone during a celebration, conducts tours of the Mescalero Apache Cultural Center. Kathleen Smith Kanseah races grandchildren up the forest road, drives a pickup truck, puts up a tent. Mildred Imach Cleghorn plays basketball, sings hymns on Wednesday nights, conducts tribal business. Ruey Haozous Darrow jets across the country, serves traditional foods out of huge pots, carefully chooses words to express herself.

These four Apache women hold their heritage in their hearts, worry that it will vanish, teach the children the old ways, and wish the young people an old-fashioned future. Each woman in this book tells about her life, remembers ancestors, and hopes for a better tomorrow. I am thankful to them for trusting that I would repeat what they said in the way they said it, and for sharing with me the indestructible, everlasting richness of the Apache culture.

To many others, my thanks as well, especially: a traveling companion and faithful friend, Louise d'A. Fairchild; a tennis partner and friend, Jane H. Cotter, whose commitment to a regular schedule of exercise for us helped the creative juices to continue flowing; friends and neighbors who looked after the house and cats, Ed and Lee Tracy; colleague Barbara R. Otto, whose wonderful sense of humor brought me much pleasure and perspective; a typist whose enthusiasm was heartwarming, Nicoli Turgate; and many friends and acquaintances whose good wishes helped sustain me through the discouraging aspects of writing a book and working full time in public welfare programs.

The late Eve Ball, noted author, scholar, and old friend, inspired me more than I can describe and continues to be my mentor in so many ways. Her irises grow in my garden, two hundred miles away from their original planting. Lynda A. Sanchez, Eve's associate, remains in touch. Angie Debo's definitive work on Geronimo encouraged me. Keith Basso, Grenville Goodwin, Harry Hoijer, Morris Opler, Doc Sonnichsen, Dan Thrapp, Don Worcester, and other writers about Apaches have my respect.

My sister, Teressa S. Matousek, visited me for ten days during the summer while I was deep in my writing. Her presence took me away from the word processor and gave me some distance from the manuscript. When I eagerly returned, I was better able to see the total book. Thanks to her for my short vacation.

A special note of thanks to one unnamed Mescalero Apache woman who declined to be part of this book. In response to a telephone call from me stating my premise and asking to interview her, she asked, "Why would I want to talk to you about anything?" After a short pause, I agreed, thanked her for her time and attention, and put the telephone down. She was the first woman I attempted to talk with and her question to me was certainly valid. Her response caused me to reexamine the entire project and eventually to redesign the hypothesis.

Certainly not to be forgotten are the folks at the University of Nevada Press and their associates who devoted professional time and attention to this book. In particular, director Thomas Radko must be acknowledged for his skill, expertise, patience, and easy manner that always smoothed a path. Copy editor Melinda Conner spent hours writing questions and directions on little yellow notes so that a high degree of quality would be assured. To these and the many other staffers, all of whom put forth their best effort, my heartfelt thanks for a job well done.

And then, these "little things" mattered: the OPEN sign on the Mescalero Apache Cultural Center's door which meant that Elbys Hugar was waiting for me; the B-R-R-U-P-P sound as I crossed the cattleguard at the beginning of the road leading to Kathleen Kanseah's house; Mildred Cleghorn's car in the driveway; and Ruey Darrow's Day-Glo chartreuse fanny pack.

Last, and with words that certainly do not, cannot, express my deep emotions, I am very grateful for the opportunity to find my own small place in the home of many Mescalero and Fort Sill Apache hearts—Whitetail.

Introduction

There is today a group of young academics loose on the land whose mission is to dispel the myths about the Old West. These scholars dispute noted western author Frederick Jackson Turner's long-lasting thesis that pioneers and cowboys defined the unique spirit of the frontier, and offer in its place what they conclude is a more realistic portrait.

According to Turner, the lure of the open frontier gave every person a chance to own property and rewarded the virtues of individualism, self-reliance, and Yankee ingenuity. This perspective has endured and grown to become the basis of countless textbooks, novels, movie and television scripts, and . . . America's international image. On the other hand, the reformers are saying that pioneer women and Oriental workers were brought to the West to facilitate white men's control, and that miners, ranchers, and cavalry troops destroyed the wilderness and the people living in it just to create what they wanted. To this theme must be added the experiences of all Native American peoples, but especially those of the Chiricahua Apache.

For no other group of American Indians was as relentlessly pursued by the armies of two countries—Mexico and the United States—as were the Chiricahua Apaches. No other group of American Indians was as denounced, as legislated against, and as hated and feared as were the Chiricahua Apaches. No other group of American Indians was imprisoned for so long as were the Chiricahua Apaches, and no other group of American Indians had an entire generation of innocent children born into captivity.

Prior to researching the background for this book, I wholeheartedly supported what I knew of the revisionist approach to American history and paid public lip service to the need for "setting the record straight." It wasn't until I became friendly with four Chiricahua Apache women, however, that I understood how seriously all Apache people had been affected by the policies of the U.S. government that "opened the West" to settlement. Once informed, I failed to remain objective, and readers may find examples of my bias here and there throughout this book. I do not apologize for my beliefs. To do so would be hypocritical and incompatible with my conscience. I have done my best, however, to convey the portraits and words of these Apaches in a pure, unadulterated manner. Throughout, they speak for themselves without interpretation or explanation from me. When relevant, background provides appropriate settings, but, in the main, the four Apache women present their own views quite ably without any prompting. They are, after all, the descendants of the Chiricahua Apache warriors and women who fought and loved, birthed and died, killed and cured, and rode and roamed the great southwestern desert and northern Mexico.

And I am a writer who focuses my research and interviews on the Chiricahua women of olden days, and on the contemporary female heirs of the Chiricahua Apache prisoners of war. Why these women rather than others? True, the Apache Nation counts a great many notable women among its prominent people, but, to me, the Chiricahua band has always been wrapped in intrigue. Through the years I learned bits and pieces about them, but the time was never right to begin a serious look into their enduring culture. Suddenly, it wouldn't wait anymore and I drove to Mescalero, more than two hundred miles from my home, and spoke to Elbys Hugar, the first Apache woman I came to know. She was open and free with her thoughts, including those about the confinement of the Chiricahua people for more than twenty-seven years.

Mildred Imach Cleghorn, another Chiricahua Apache woman, was a prisoner for the first four years of her life, until she and her family were released. Her father, Richard Imach, had been a child himself when first confined by the U.S. military. Her mother, Amy Wratten, was also a prisoner, even though she was the child of a white interpreter and his Apache wife. Mrs. Cleghorn is now the chairperson of the Fort Sill Apache Tribe, was the 1989 Indian of the Year, and has always been a natural leader of her people. She is, at eighty years of age, a truly beautiful woman in all aspects of her being. Even as she speaks the language of her captors and functions as an equal, she remains faithful to the origins of her people. None of the other three Apache women I interviewed for this book had the same experience, but all have listened to stories about the way it was when they were a free people, when they were not free, and when they were, at long last, free again.

Elbys Naiche Hugar, the great-granddaughter of Cochise, speaks lovingly of her youth lived atop a mountain, when her family, the descendants of one of the greatest Apaches of all times, was financially impoverished but emotionally enriched. Mrs. Hugar's spiritual power is so striking that it can practically be touched. Today, she is the curator of the Mescalero Apache Cultural Center and serves, informally through her work, as the unofficial Apache ambassador to the world.

Kathleen Smith Kanseah, the descendant of a Mexican woman captured as a child more than one hundred years ago by the Apaches, recalls being able to attend school with white children only because her mother worked for the government. She continued her education, became a medical professional, and is today teaching her grandchildren the ancient Apache customs and traditions. While Mrs. Kanseah acknowledges the girls' need to become part of the larger society, she will not stand idly by and permit the beauty and strength of her culture to be assimilated into the melting pot's anonymity.

Ruey Haozous Darrow is a career woman who travels extensively throughout the central and southwestern regions of the nation for the Indian Health Service. She is intelligent, independent, and sophisticated. In her heart and in her spirit she is first and foremost an Apache woman. One of five living children of Apache prisoners of war, Mrs. Darrow, despite an affliction caused by a childhood battle with infantile paralysis, still wraps herself in an Apache shawl and, in great pain, dances around the fire with the *Gah'e*, the Mountain Spirit dancers, to honor the Apache way.

Other Apache women in this book can only be described: Dahteste, a woman sent by Geronimo to meet with U.S. Army officers in a first attempt at a negotiated surrender; Gouyen, the avenger who settled the score with Comanches for her husband's death; Ishton, the lovely wife of Chief Juh who was killed with her baby daughter in a cavalry attack; Siki, called Tsa-i-ka in Apache, whose thousand-mile journey on foot led her out of Mexican slavery and back to her people; Lozen, the unique medicine woman and warrior whose remarkable power helped keep the Apaches free for as long as possible; and Blossom Wratten Haozous, a prisoner of war and also a contemporary woman whose commitment to education greatly influenced her family.

There were other Apache women, of course, whose contributions to the history of their people will never be known, and some whose efforts died with them. Many Apache women are buried where they fell with an American soldier's bullet in their bodies. Others, like Geronimo's first family, lay aboveground, untouched, in the spot where they had been slaughtered by the Mexican army. After imprisonment, Apache women were buried, some in unmarked graves, in Florida, in Alabama, or in the cemetery on the Fort Sill, Oklahoma, grounds—all places where they had been confined for almost thirty years. Most epitaphs are simple—too simple—and fail miserably to pay any tribute to the women at all.

Modern Apache women, however, honor their ancestors every day through their actions, their activities, and their respect for the customs and traditions of their heritage. Mildred Cleghorn holds the banner high as she meets with officials on every level of government—federal, state, and local—in an attempt to bring services and programs to members of her tribe. Elbys Hugar greets people from around the world at the Mescalero Apache Cultural Center and is painstakingly meticulous in explaining the Apache life, lest there be the slightest misunderstanding. Kathleen Kanseah perpetuates tradition in the hearts and minds of children so that Apache ways cannot, must not, disappear. Ruey Darrow shares her heritage through photographs so a researcher can see for herself the faces of the people whose names and experiences she has come to know.

And today's Apache women are also speaking out. There is much to say. In clear, crisp voices on these pages they state the truth, tell their own stories, and repeat the old ways as they heard them described by their mothers, their grandmothers, their great-grandmothers. These Apache women look from the past to the future and, as intermediaries, convey the tribe's history to the next generation, just as Apache women have always done. They are the last generation to hear and learn directly from the elders about the treatment Apache people suffered in prison, afterward, and, in some cases, even today.

Changing the nation's perception about the frontier West is a difficult task at best, but one that must be done if American history is to be honored and not perpetuated in its current format. The new version must include the injustices committed against all Native Americans who, from their perspective, defended and protected their homelands against escalating encroachment. A special chapter should be dedicated to the Chiricahua Apache, certainly one of the most valiant indigenous peoples of the Southwest. That this group was accorded the worst treatment of any Native Americans by the U.S. government is evidence of America's hard-gotten respect for Apache power. That the Apache people still, more than a century after the last surrender, maintain a formidable reputation, is testimony to their continuing independence and individuality.

Revisionist American history incorporates a point of view different from the usual approach. As the twenty-first century nears, the time may be right to let more facts become known about the events that transpired on the plains, in the mountains, and on the deserts of the West hundreds of years ago. After centuries of lies and half-truths, our country should be mature enough to accept a new truth about itself, but then again, it might still be too soon for America's pen to be mightier than its sword.

Not
So
Long
Ago

1

In the beginning, when no human beings were alive, the flood subsided and the clouds drew mountains up out of the water. Birds and animals moved into the mountains to find a good place to live. Child-of-the-Water, a supernatural being, stood in a certain place, caused a dark cloud to form above him, and said he was going back to the sky. The cloud encircled him, and when it disappeared, Child-of-the-Water was gone. In his place were two human beings, one of whom was called Changing Woman and the other, suddenly reappearing, was Child-of-the-Water himself. From these, the Apache people have sprung.[1]

This is a creation myth, a fable used by members of the Chiricahua band of Apaches to teach others how things happened. Different bands within the tribe at large may have different explanations regarding their origin.

The Chiricahua, however, rely on Changing Woman and Child-of-the-Water.

Chiricahua is a name given by unknown individuals or groups a long time ago to a band of Apaches living in Arizona's Chiricahua Mountains. One of the most courageous Apache warriors, Geronimo, called the Chiricahua by their Apache name, Chokonen, and identified himself as belonging to another band, or subtribe, the Bedonkohe, who inhabited a region "west from the east line of Arizona and south from the headwaters of the Gila River."[2] The Chiricahua themselves say that at one time "the entire tribe lived in the vicinity of Hot Springs, New Mexico, and that from here they spread south and west and differentiated into bands."[3]

There were other Apaches in the region as well: the Northern Tonto, the Southern Tonto, the White Mountain, and San Carlos bands. These groups have their own generic name, Western Apache Subtribal Groups, and their own customs and traditions. However, a century or more ago, all Apaches knew about each other and communicated. They shared rituals, traditions, and terrain, to say nothing of the hardships they experienced in common. Today, the Chiricahua Apache people live mainly in two states—New Mexico and Oklahoma. The New Mexicans reside on the Mescalero Apache Reservation in the southeastern portion of the state, in the shadow of a sacred mountain known as Sierra Blanca. The Oklahoma Chiricahuas do not live on a reservation. Instead, they reside in and near a town named Apache.

Apache creation myths are numerous, but they are not dramatically distinct from many other cultures' versions of their beginnings—including the Christian myth of Adam and Eve in the Garden of Eden. In fact, the reference to the flood may show some Christian influence, as does a statement made by one member of the Chiricahua Apache band when discussing his origin. "There was a world before this one, according to the old Indians," he said, "and it was destroyed by water. All the people living before this world were washed out."[4]

Creation myths form the center of a society's system of beliefs. They make things seem plausible; they satisfy; they interpret.[5] They don't have to be logical and they don't have to be similar, but they all have been handed down from the elders through the generations, usually in story-telling format.

Geronimo recalled another rendition of the Apache creation myth. More than a century ago he told an interviewer that he understood there was a battle between the birds and the beasts, the former wanting light and the latter wanting darkness.[6] After the war was over and the birds were victorious, only a few human beings were alive. One of them was Changing Woman, called White Painted Woman by Geronimo. Years later she bore a son whom she hid in a cave lest the one beast remaining alive, a dragon, should find and devour her beloved boy. The disaster almost happened, but the boy finally defeated the dragon with a bow and arrows and was then named Apache. The almighty Giver of Life, called USSEN by the Apache people, taught the boy how to prepare herbs for medicine, how to hunt, and how to fight. The youngster wore eagle feathers as a sign of justice, wisdom, and power.[7]

In 1884 John G. Bourke recorded a complicated creation myth of the Apache people involving twelve deities, twelve black winds, twelve heavens, twelve suns, twelve moons, and twelve parts to the earth. Other winds—green, blue, yellow, and white—were involved in the creation of the world also, but Child-of-the-Dawn, a deity, played a major part, as did a ray of sun that shone down on the earth and formed a white stone. Other sunbeams did the same, and before long, each rock brought forth a pair of human beings. From the male, called Child-of-the-Water, all the nations of the earth were derived.[8]

Through stories like these, children in every society learn who they are and what is expected of them; Jack and Jill, for example, teach youngsters to be careful lest they fall. Pinocchio warns not to lie, or noses will grow. The list of examples of good and bad behavior, as well as reasons for being and other basic truths, conveyed in every culture through the use of storytelling is endless.

In Native American societies, storytelling was and still is a winter activity. In olden days children and adults spent evenings around a fire, wrapped in warm robes, talking about their beginnings and learning or relearning why things are the way they are. In this way Chiricahua Apache children heard the creation myths and also were taught practical matters: the characteristics of the land that sustained them and how to honor it and survive on it, respect for their elders, games to play, how to whittle a bow and arrows, how to weave baskets, and other information important—from a cultural perspective—for youngsters to know. The Chiricahua Apaches were Cochise's band, and he, everyone knew, was a proud, striking, and fearless leader. According to U.S. Army records, Cochise was tall and well proportioned with dark eyes and a pleasant expression.[9] One personal account reports his height at five feet ten inches,

> in person lithe and wiry, every muscle being well developed and firm. A silver thread was now and then visible in his otherwise black hair which he wore straight cut around his head about on a level with his chin. His countenance displayed great force of character, and his expression was a little sad. He spoke with great ease.[10]

One Apache leader described Cochise as "physically and mentally superior. . . . According to our standards, he was a very handsome man."[11]

It is easy to imagine boys and girls around a fire, bundled up and growing sleepy listening to winter tales, then seeing Cochise approach. Quickly becoming alert at the sight of the enormous, powerful chief, the children might have paid just a bit more attention to an instruction that night about marriage, for example, and how unmarried girls, carefully guarded by relatives, meet young men. Or the children might have learned what gifts must be exchanged between the young couple's families when an agreement to marry has been reached.[12]

In those days, many marriages were too short because of the violence experienced by the Apache people. In the middle 1800s, while Cochise was chief of the Chiricahuas, there had been a Spanish and Mexican military presence in the Southwest for years. Then the Americans arrived. Naturally, the Apaches forcefully resisted any encroachment by strangers into the territory that once was solely their terrain. More often than not, Apache losses were more substantial than were their enemies' defeats, so it was crucial for young people to marry and have children immediately. It was logical that if the numbers of people lost in battle or through illness, accidents, and infant mortality could be replaced by an increase in the number of children being born into the tribe, the Apaches would not disappear. The tribe, after all, had been a part of the land longer than the non-native newcomers who arrogantly considered the Southwest to belong to them.

The date of the Apaches' arrival in the Southwest is not known for certain, but one chronicler of the early Apache presence wrote that it was "about the year 1560 that the first Apache came from the south in a large band and joined the Navajo."[13] Apaches were in the Southwest when the Spanish arrived in the 1500s, and they had carried their customs and traditions with them, especially those sacred rituals and ceremonies that were necessary to ensure a maiden's preparation for the future.

For an Apache girl, the path to marriage and childbearing started with a puberty ceremony honoring White Painted Woman, the revered deity who has control over fertility and is the essence of long life.[14] The puberty ceremony, according to a Western Apache creation myth, is also hope for perpetual youth, abundance, and good health. "There was a time when White Painted Woman lived all alone," the legend declares.

> Longing for children, she slept with the Sun and not long after gave birth to Slayer of Monsters, the foremost culture hero. Four days later, White Painted Woman became pregnant by water and gave birth to Born-of-Water (also known as Child-of-the-Water). As Slayer of Monsters and Child-of-the-Water matured, White Painted Woman instructed them on how to live. Then they left home and, following her advice, rid the earth of most of its evil. White Painted Woman never became old. When she reached an advanced age, she walked toward the east. After a while, she saw herself coming toward herself. When she came together, there was only one, the young one. Then she was like a young girl all over again. Thus the power of White Painted Woman offered the pubescent girl longevity and the physical capabilities of someone perpetually young.[15]

White Painted Woman also told the Chiricahua,

> We will have the girls' puberty rite. When the girls first menstruate, you shall have a feast. There shall be songs for the girls. During this feast, the *Gah'e* [masked dancers who imitate the sacred mountain

spirits] shall dance in front. After that there shall be round dancing and face to face dancing.[16]

Puberty ceremonies were (and still are) a joyful, essential, and spiritual part of becoming an adult female Apache and were held, with variations, by each band of the tribe. Thomas Mails, in some of the most complete descriptions on record, portrayed the Western Apache puberty ceremony as being comprised of eight distinct parts or phases, each with its own name.[17] Still today, the primary objective of the ceremony is to celebrate a young girl's entrance into womanhood, which ensures the continuation of the tribe, and to prepare her for a useful and abundant life. "That's been the intention all along," said Evelyn Breuninger, a member of the Mescalero Apache Tribal Council and chairman of the council's Community Services Subcommittee, "to wish them a good life, good family, good child-bearing years—everything that goes along with being a woman."[18]

In phase I of the Western Apache puberty ceremony, which has been recorded extensively, the girl dances alone while chants sung by others describe the creation and the blessings bestowed on the Apache people by White Painted Woman. Harry Hoijer painstakingly recorded some of these songs more than fifty years ago and was one of the first authors to document, bilingually, the sacred Apache chants.[19] Phase II re-creates White Painted Woman's impregnation by the sun. The girl kneels on a buckskin, raises her hands to her shoulders, and rocks back and forth, symbolizing the posture in which White Painted Woman experienced her first menstrual period. The girl's sponsor, an important woman in this ceremony, dances beside her. In phase III the sponsor massages the girl so that her soft body can be molded into straightness, beauty, and strength. Phase IV includes patterns of running, symbolizing a stage of life through which the girl will pass. In phase V the girl runs faster, like White Painted Woman, without getting tired. The medicine man blesses the girl in phase VI and pours a small basket of candy, corn kernels, and coins over her head, symbolizing food, good crops, and enough money for the future. During phase VII the girl and her sponsor dance in place before phase VIII, when she will throw a buckskin, used throughout the ceremony, to the east, meaning that there will always be meat in her camp and good hunting for everyone. She also throws blankets to the other cardinal directions, assuring that she will always have warmth and that her camp will always be clean. The Western Apache puberty ceremony is concluded after phase VIII, but White Painted Woman's power is thought to reside in the girl for four days and may be used to heal or bring rain during that time.[20] Adaptations and variations of this puberty ceremony have occurred throughout the history of the Apache people, regardless of whether they were free or imprisoned by the U.S. government.]

In 1886 two warriors, Geronimo and Naiche (son of Cochise), and the less than fifty people with them became the last Apaches to surrender to the military. Twenty-seven years of imprisonment in Florida, Alabama, and Fort Sill, Oklahoma, followed, with many of the great chiefs, warriors, and others (including many children) forced to live and die far from their homes in the desert Southwest. Finally, in 1913, four years after Geronimo's death in captivity, the government allowed the Chiricahua Apache people to leave Fort Sill. Of these, 183 ex-prisoners resettled in New Mexico at Whitetail, a remote area of the Mescalero Apache Reservation; 78 others decided to remain in the vicinity of Fort Sill. Almost one thousand miles west of Oklahoma, the Western Apache bands, never captives like the Chiricahua, were still free and living on reservations. They were never forced to leave their original homeland.[21] The policymakers in Washington, D.C., focused their attention on the Chiricahua band because it was they who broke out almost yearly and caused uproars. Other Apache bands were never considered as troublesome and apparently didn't represent as much of a threat to settlers and citizens as did the Chiricahua.

The Chiricahua continued the puberty rite through the years, regardless of where they were—warring with the Spanish, Mexican, or American armies, in captivity, on reservations, or living among others. On the Mescalero Apache Reservation, for example, the 1936 ceremony in which three young women participated was described by Anne Pence Davis and subsequently published in *New Mexico*, the state's official magazine.[22] Davis recorded the puberty rite legend as beginning with the grandfather of the gods giving Old Woman a message for her people, the Apaches. The message itself conveyed the reason for the ritual. Old Woman found it difficult to keep up with other members of the Apache Tribe as they followed the

Two Presbyterian missionaries visit aged Apache woman, 1898. (Courtesy of Western History Collections, University of Oklahoma Library, photo no. 195)

buffalo and other sources of food. Finally, exhausted, she fell by the way-side and the others moved on without her. She slept and fell into a coma. Suddenly, a constant jingling penetrated her deathlike state and caused her to become instantly alert. She heard a spirit voice that described the process of the puberty rite and urged her to hurry and rejoin her tribe so she could instruct them. Revivified, Old Woman followed the directions.[23]

Dan Nicholas, a full-blooded Apache living at Mescalero in 1939, wrote an article about the puberty ceremony in response to a request from the parents of two girls for whom the ceremony was to be conducted.[24] Nicholas said that the puberty rite was given to the people by the Giver of Life through Esdzanadeha, or White Painted Woman. Beautiful Esdzana-deha reared her son, Killer of Enemies, in spite of several monsters who were depopulating the earth at that time. Her son killed the monsters to make the world safe for the Apache people, and because of this Esdzanadeha is revered. According to Nicholas, during the four-day puberty ceremony each of the girls is likened to Esdzanadeha, and the same songs sung in praise of White Painted Woman are repeated throughout the rite. Nicholas detailed the ceremony quite carefully and placed great emphasis on the role of the medicine men who are essential to the ritual.

C. L. Sonnichsen concluded that

> the drums and songs, the sacred yellow pollen on her cheeks and forehead, the gifts and congratulations of her friends and relatives, the feasting and good fellowship—all made the puberty ceremony a happy and solemn occasion for a Mescalero girl. It made her think seriously of her responsibilities and of her obligations to the power that gives and takes away.[25]

To honor this power and White Painted Woman, during the puberty ceremony Mescalero girls wear an elaborate buckskin dress modeled after the one worn by White Painted Woman. Symbols are painted or beaded onto the top of the dress by grandmothers, well in advance of the ritual and in conjunction with the girl's sponsor, a woman carefully selected to instruct and accompany the girl through the sacred rite and to paint her body yellow with pollen—considered a fertilizing color—and red to symbolize blood and life.[26]

Mails, describing the maiden's special dress, wrote that it was made, in the early days, from five doeskins or buckskins with a tail of a black-tailed doe suspended from the back hem of the top.[27] The symbols on the dress or on the girl's body included the morning star, the crescent moon, a stepped design for the puberty dwelling (a place especially designated for the girl's use during the rite), circles for the sun, and arcs for the rainbow. The dress was blessed by having someone sing for it, usually an old woman who began her songs as long as two months in advance of the scheduled ceremony. The woman was paid for her services, a tradition once based in commodities or other treasures but now quite costly. Mails also reported that the cost (in 1974) might exceed $750, and at that time had become a ceremony that not all Apache families could afford.[28] A more recent (1989) estimate is $8,000–$10,000 when one tallies all the expenses, including the cost of feeding many family members, guests, and outside visitors for four days. As a result, approximately one out of three young women eligible for the public puberty ceremony actually experiences it.[29] Other families may have private ceremonies for their daughters, and there are also some families today who ignore the traditional ways.

Theoretically and practically, the ancient puberty rite shows Apache girls the way toward a good life by its emphasis on four all-important life objectives: "physical strength, a good disposition, prosperity, and a sound, healthy, uncrippled old age."[30] But regardless of whether or not she participates in the ritual, an Apache girl begins preparation for marriage and childbearing and for her future role as an adult woman and mother when her first menstrual period arrives. Often, in older days, the young woman needed to be adequately prepared for all possible events. Her life would not be easy.

In their traditional roles, Apache women led hard lives. The phases associated with massage and running in the puberty ceremony symbolically provided the young woman with the physical strength needed for the adult tasks ahead: gathering food; the demands of planting, irrigating, and harvesting the crops; providing and preparing large amounts of food for extended family members; building protective shelters; finding and hauling firewood on her back in the fall and winter; and giving birth to healthy babies.

"Women were the basic components around which a social unit was structured," said Apache historian Michael Darrow. A Fort Sill Apache himself, Darrow has spent several years studying the history of his people.

> The woman and her family, her daughters, her daughters' husbands would constitute a family group and they would live not as individual families, but would live in family units. Grandparents, all of their children, and whatever relatives happen to be around. . . . Anthropologists have said that the Apaches had a patriarchal society, but it was only superficially patriarchal. The women had an extreme amount of power in the decision making process.[31]

A good disposition, believed to be one of the gifts Changing Woman confers, promises that the Apache girl will always have the support and assistance of her relatives. This is a crucial concept in traditional culture. Much of Apache life depends on goodwill among relatives. Nonrelatives are approached with caution in all affairs because of the timeless Apache fear of witchcraft. It is an accepted presumption among some Apaches that relatives will not bewitch relatives, but the same cannot be promised for others.[32] Through participating in the puberty ceremony the girl inherits a pleasant personality and other admirable traits of character that will protect her against bewitchment and ensure a smooth and happy path through life, one that is rich with blessings.

In olden times, one measure of affluence was in terms of the abundance of food. The puberty ceremony promised freedom from hunger because so many events affected prosperity—drought, torrential rains, frost, lightning, bewitchment. Having sufficient food was never guaranteed; but the phase of the puberty ceremony in which the girl dances on the buckskin transmitted a promise that she would always have an adequate supply of meat, despite the ever-present danger of conditions beyond individual control.

The Apache culture acknowledges, however, that many external conditions may not respect devout behavior. Preparation for the unexpected was necessary, and acceptance of fate was especially important in the days when epidemic diseases were devastating Native American populations, when the Spanish, Mexican, and American armies were pursuing Apaches, and when pregnancy and childbirth endangered a mother's life. Personal power acquired through the puberty ceremony was thought to assist the maiden in overcoming tribulations associated with those adversities and others such as accidents, bad weather, hunger, and so on. Thus her life would be prolonged as a result of the ritual, and living to an old age was viewed as evidence of victory over all the dark forces in the universe designed to do harm.[33] Staying on good terms with the spirit world by observing and honoring taboos, such as grinding corn in a certain manner, taking care that water never fell on an eagle feather, and praying on occasions like the birth of a child, when a new shelter was built, before the hunt, and before a long journey helped ensure that the girl would reach the respected status of an elder.[34] All along the way, the puberty ceremony was her benefactor.

Rev. Robert Schut, pastor of the Mescalero Reformed Church, said of the ceremony:

> I think that the idea of the ceremony is one of the most beautiful things that could ever happen. Imagine this: for twelve days—four days precelebration, four days of the celebration, and four days following—this girl is a special person. All this time, the family and the community is praying for her. It's very spiritual. . . . I look at that and think it's something that every kid in the world should grow up with. . . . I don't know if there's anything comparable in the white dominant society.[35]

The Mescalero Reformed Church was originally organized on the Mescalero Reservation in early 1909 with nineteen members. In 1913 membership was increased with the addition of eighty-nine Chiricahua Apaches who moved from Fort Sill to Whitetail and had their church membership transferred from the mission in Oklahoma.

In a matriarchal society such as the Apache, one might assume that women would take a leading role in religious activities. But in the Reformed Church of Mescalero, both men and women participate actively in leadership today. More than seventy-five years ago, Chiricahua chief Naiche, the son of Cochise, and Eugene Chihuahua, son of Chiricahua chief Chihuahua, became elders in the church, as did other former warriors and scouts, all of whom were converted to Protestantism through the efforts of early missionaries at Fort Sill. The Reformed church was the choice of Geronimo during the last years of his life, but he eventually was dropped from the rolls because he drank too much. Today, approximately eighty families participate in the continuing ministry at Mescalero and about a hundred attend Sunday worship. The youth ministry consists of a high school group of between ten and twelve teenagers and a junior high school group of about sixteen youngsters. Young Apaches are participating in youth activities in increasing numbers.

When asked specifically about the women in the church, Rev. Schut talked about hearing their voices rise as the congregation sings hymns in

Apache Indian camp in Arizona. (Courtesy of Smithsonian Institution, National Anthropological Archives, negative no. 44, 820-G)

English and Apache, and about the devout spirituality he sees among all parishioners as they pray.

> Women are part of the leadership. We have always had at least one woman on our church board. There have been more men than women, which again is somewhat unusual in an Indian community. . . . As I hear some of our older Indian ladies pray, many times it will be in Apache, but they'll throw in an English word every now and then. They'll pray, even at Bible study. They'll pray for every member of their family by name, and five to ten minutes at prayer is no time at all.[36]

Apache women have been reverent throughout their history; they have a long heritage of spirituality. "All Apache mothers teach their children to pray," recorded author Eve Ball during a conversation with Daklugie, a noted Apache leader and son of the Nednhi band's Chief Juh and his wife, Geronimo's beloved sister Ishton.[37]

Prayer and praying is the basis of an all-pervasive spirituality that characterizes Apache people and is kept alive by the women of the tribe through at least one of their roles—instructors of the children. For example, a mother might teach her child about the hunt, an activity Rev. Schut cites as an illustration of Apache spirituality. In many other cultures, hunting is sport and partakers must obtain permission to participate through an agency or an organization responsible for its regulation. In those societies, hunting may be intended to cull the herd, to challenge machismo, or to reinforce a so-called primitive bond. But to the Apaches, stalking game through the forest is a spiritual experience. "They just tie all of life together," said Rev. Schut of the Apache people.[38]

Hunting is an activity similar to the raids or war parties of the days when the Apaches freely roamed the Southwest. Then, women who stayed at home "could help contribute to the success of the enterprise and, equally important, take steps to assure the party's safe return" by praying every morning for four days after the men left, including while cooking, taking meat off the fire, and stirring the fire's ashes.[39] Taboos were also a part of spirituality; for example, when the men returned from a hunt, a pregnant wife would not eat the intestines or calves of a deer's leg. If she did, it was believed that her husband's arrows would not follow a straight path the next time he went hunting.[40] These and other prohibitions were solemnly respected and considered sacred, rather than just the customary obligations of a dutiful wife.

On the other hand, cooking was part of a Chiricahua woman's chores and was the natural extension of several different activities, most especially the gathering of food. As a girl matured, she accompanied women of the camp on expeditions of food gathering. Older women supervised, answered questions, trained the girls, and taught them to identify various plants and how to shell, hull, husk, and strip wild foods to obtain the edible parts. Climatic conditions and seasonal changes dictated the availability of various foods that would supplement and, in times of scarcity or distant travel, supplant meat brought home by the men. Mescal, an Apache staple produced by century plants, was gathered by women and stored after it was sun dried and preserved by painting it with a thin layer of mescal juice. When it was to be cooked, the mescal was soaked in water and its stalks and crowns were cut, roasted in pits, and then mixed with berries and nuts, some of which had been packed away with wild onions the women had picked the year before.

Apache women made soup from white roots and tubers boiled with chunks of meat. The white flowers of the yucca cactus were also boiled, dried, and stored. Unopened yucca buds were split and dried as sweetening for hot herbal teas. Seeds, wild raspberries and strawberries, acorns, beans, chokecherries, and potatoes were available and picked or dug up, either to be prepared right away or stored for future consumption. Acorns were mixed with meat and fat, rolled into a ball, and given to the men to take on hunts or raids.

Wild grasses and crushed potatoes formed a flour that served as the basis for bread, which often contained ground berries and beans as well. Honey was spread on the bread, too. It was removed directly from the comb after smudge fires had smoked the bees out. Arrows shot by women or young boys tore off chunks of the hive, which were squeezed until the honey dripped into bags. Women also collected wild tobacco while in search of food. Most everyone except youngsters smoked by rolling the raw tobacco in oak leaves.[41]

In short, then, women were responsible for many of the day-to-day activities that allowed the tribe to function as a unit. As Donald Cole summarized it,

> Men were not thought able to survive for any extended time without the presence of women to provide the necessary functions of gathering and preserving. Women, however, were thought capable of living for extended time periods without the presence or assistance of men.[42]

When Apache women had to walk far from home or camp to find food, they were accompanied by certain men whose job it was to protect them from all human and animal dangers. If a destination was nearby, however, a woman went by herself or with a friend. Only medicine women usually traveled far alone or with a young apprentice. One Apache medicine woman, Captain Jack, loved to instruct her grandchildren "in the prayers and invocations to the gods worshiped by her fathers" as she roamed the land in search of healing herbs.[43] Another medicine woman, Tze-go-juni, was a Chiricahua with a long history of captivity by the Mexicans. She had also been mangled by a mountain lion and struck by lightning. Just surviving these ordeals as she lived her life and practiced her healing gave her great influence within her band. Around her neck she wore an amulet shaped like a spear point, made of quartz taken from a ledge at the foot of a tree that had also been struck by lightning. "A tiny piece was broken off and ground into the finest powder and administered in water to women during the time of gestation," reported John Bourke.[44] Bourke also wrote that Apache medicine women devoted themselves solely to obstetrics, but subsequent information about the woman warrior Lozen, also considered to be a medicine woman, and other healers has added more dimensions to his conclusions, which were recorded in the years 1887–1888.[45]

Medicine women and medicine men were essential to the spiritual and ceremonial lives of the Apache people. They brought healing to the tribe and were directly connected with the spirit world. Geronimo was a powerful medicine man to whom USSEN spoke on a regular basis. On one especially important occasion, Geronimo went to Chief Juh's camp to officiate as medicine man when Ishton was giving birth. The women in Geronimo's family had a history of difficult pregnancies and even more difficult childbirths. When Geronimo knew Ishton's time had come, he risked his life traveling through hostile territory to be at his sister's side. For four days he called upon his powers to help Ishton, but she labored and suffered terribly without relief. Finally, Geronimo climbed a mountain to plead with USSEN for Ishton's life. Arms and eyes upraised, he begged for her well-being with heartfelt words. USSEN answered, telling the warrior/medicine man that Ishton and the baby would live and that he, Geronimo, would die a natural death at a very old age.[46] When Geronimo returned to Ishton, she had given birth and all was well. Geronimo lived to be nearly eighty years old; he died of pneumonia in 1909 while still a prisoner at Fort Sill.

Apache women frequently had to fight alone or beside the men for their lives, regardless of their physical condition. Eugene Chihuahua, son of Chief Chihuahua, related an incident that happened to a woman when Eugene was a young man. The U.S. Cavalry was following some Apache men but left troopers to find the missing women and children. There was quite a bit of shooting, and the soldiers finally dragged a woman, wounded in the leg, out of her hiding place in a cave. They forced her and others, including the young Eugene, to march to the nearest fort, a distance of many miles. Eugene found a stick that the woman could use as a cane or leg brace until they got to the buildings in which they were confined. There, food was thrown on the ground for the Apache prisoners to eat. The woman received no medical attention. Instead, she was put to work digging a latrine for the soldiers. She bound her walking stick to her leg and worked as hard as she could . . . for many days. One day she fell over and could not be roused, even by repeated prods from a soldier's rifle butt and kicks from his boots. "We knew that she had escaped and gone to the Happy Place, and we were glad," said Eugene Chihuahua.[47]

During more peaceful times, however, customary social behavior was observed in which Apache women took subordinate roles. Mails has recorded that only in very few activities such as drinking, dancing, and gambling was an Apache woman equal to her husband. In most of their actions together, despite the matriarchal society, the husband and his wishes and needs dominated. As an example, after preparing a meal a woman waited until her husband had eaten before she finished what he left as her meal. Also, she was expected to bring him his horse and saddle and carry water for the family in a large bottle she wove of grasses and reeds. The vessel was smeared with pine pitch, inside and out, to make it watertight. She carried the bottle on her back and supported it by a strap across her forehead. Additionally, an Apache woman was responsible for carrying wood in a large basket on her back, also with a strap over her forehead. Frequently, this basket was quite heavy and stacked high with large and small sticks for the fire that she was expected to build.[48]

Apache life sometimes included vindictive acts. Goodwin and Basso reported that if an Apache woman lost a loved one in battle, a future war party would avenge the killing by bringing back a captive for the woman to kill. "The woman in charge had the first shot," an informant told the researchers. "Then after her, each woman had a chance shooting, or with a spear, to see who would finally kill him. But they never scalped the captive. They just buried the body because if they didn't, it would stink."[49]

Apache women carrying wood.
(Courtesy of Arizona Historical Society Library/Tucson, negative no. 58632)

Education of the children was a major duty of a mother and her female relations. At the age of puberty, most boys were taken from their mothers and trained in masculine endeavors by their fathers; women remained solely responsible for instructing their daughters in such skills as preparing the meats brought back from a hunt, tanning hides and making them into clothing, and basket weaving.[50]

An Apache woman could expect to be beaten by her husband for any infraction of his rules; a woman who committed adultery ran the risk of having her nose cut off at its tip by her enraged husband . . . if she were caught.[51]

Mescalero Apache medicine women had additional duties along with their regular chores. They were present when a young boy took his first smoke; they supervised a baby's first haircut and the initial wearing of moccasins when a baby took its first few steps. They said prayers over a child at birth and put pollen on a baby's forehead when the child was first put onto a cradleboard,[52] the apparatus used by many generations of Apache women to rock, carry, and rest their children. Sadly, a cradleboard swinging from a tree might also indicate that the baby wrapped so securely inside was dead.

It was so easy to become married in prereservation days that most Apache babies were probably born within a marriage. Gordon Baldwin reported that

> the average age at marriage was fifteen to eighteen for women, twenty to twenty-five for men. Young men would not get married quite as early because they first had to prove their ability to provide for a family by taking part in at least four raids.[53]

According to tradition, Apache males were allowed more than one wife, but when there were several wives, each of a husband's families occupied separate living quarters.

John C. Cremony, one of the earliest observers of Apache ways, reported,

> A celebrated warrior, and one wise in the traditions of his people, told me that time was when only one woman was deemed the proper share of one man, but their losses by war and other causes had so reduced the number of males that it was judged politic to make a change in this custom.[54]

These changes must have occurred before Geronimo reached marriageable age, because it is said that he had nine wives altogether, although not simultaneously. His first wife, Alope, their three children, and his mother were brutally murdered by Mexicans who rode into an Apache camp while the warriors were trading in a nearby town. All of Geronimo's life from that time forward was filled with a hatred for Mexicans, and he took revenge many times over for the slaughter of his family.

Geronimo remembered the tragedy and described it to S. M. Barrett as he dictated his reminiscences in 1906.

> Late one afternoon when returning from town we were met by a few women and children who told us that Mexican troops from

"Nal-tzuci-ei-ah"
Apache Squaw. Spy in Chiricahua Campaign.

Nal-Tzuci-ei-ah, or "Cut Nose." Apache custom dictated that the tip of a woman's nose be cut off if she committed adultery.
(Courtesy of Arizona Historical Society/Tucson, negative no. 25633)

One method of Apache infant burial: cradleboard hanging from tree.
(Courtesy of Smithsonian Institution, National Anthropological Archives,
negative no. T-12314)

some other town had attacked our camp, killed all the warriors of the guard, captured all our ponies, secured our arms, destroyed our supplies, and killed many of our women and children. Quickly we separated, concealing ourselves as best we could until nightfall, when we assembled at our appointed place of rendezvous—a thicket by the river. Silently we stole in one by one, sentinels were placed, and when all were counted, I found that my aged mother, my young wife, and my three small children were among the slain. . . . I had no weapon, nor did I hardly wish to fight, neither did I contemplate recovering the bodies of my loved ones, for that was forbidden.[55]

A contemporary author, Edwin R. Sweeney, believes that the older Geronimo's recollections can be trusted "only in part. . . . He lost his family but not, it would seem, at the time and place, or under the circumstances he described when he dictated his autobiography . . . and in his desire to present himself as an innocent victim, he ignored the long series of raids and reprisals which preceded Carrasco's attack. It is hard to believe that he was not involved with them."[56]

One of Geronimo's wives was a woman named Francesca, who, in her youth, had a bloody battle with a mountain lion. The animal "clawed her scalp partly from her head and tore her face."[57] Despite her serious injuries, Francesca was able to stab the lion until it was dead, and then the two women with her replaced her scalp and bound it with buckskin thongs. The women took sputum from the dead lion and rubbed it into Francesca's wounds. Then they cut nopal leaves, burned off the thorns, split them, and applied the fleshy side to Francesca's head. She survived but was scarred for life and thought she would never marry because she had become so ugly. Geronimo believed she deserved a good husband because "she was the bravest of all Apache women," and so he married her.[58] There is no further mention of her or of their marriage. She may be buried near his grave at the Fort Sill Apache Cemetery, although the marker carries no designation of her relationship to Geronimo. As a matter of fact, the grave is removed from the other members of his family and the name on the marker is "Francisco." The epitaph, however, reads "Apache woman."

Multiple wives presented no problem insofar as cultural mores were concerned. As an example, the culture prescribed adaptations to the situation with regard to housing and these customs were carefully observed. As a prisoner of war at Mount Vernon, Alabama (before being moved to Fort Sill),

> Geronimo and his two wives occupied a two-room log cabin that was located in the center of the village. . . . Wife Zi-yeh and her daughter Eva and son Fenton slept in one room while the second wife, Ih-tedda and daughter Lenna (Marion) occupied the other room.[59]

In prereservation days, Apache wives of leaders like Geronimo and Naiche were expected to take leadership positions, regardless of how many women were married to the same man. These women organized food-gathering expeditions, set good examples for other women to follow, and exercised quite a bit of authority. They were permitted to speak at war dances and at chiefs' councils. Along with all other Apache women, they owned personal property and had some voice in family affairs. However, regardless of all of these activities, and even though descent was traced through their bloodlines, many Apache women continued to be treated by their husbands as subordinate to men. But there were ways of relief. If a husband was too demanding, an Apache woman could easily divorce him. All she had to do was put his belongings outside their home, and they were no longer married. In those cases the husband went back to his mother and began looking for another wife. If the husband was the partner seeking a divorce, he would tell his wife he was going hunting and then never return.[60]

Married couples shared and enjoyed a popular Apache myth about the trickster, Coyote, and two newborn fawns he came across during his travels. The babies were good looking and Coyote wanted his offspring to look like them, rather than like him. He found their mother, Doe, and asked her how she did it. "Put your children in a little cleft in the rocks, cover them up with juniper branches, and set fire to the wood. When the wood pops and crackles, that will give your children spots," she slyly advised. Well, the old trickster did just that and got tricked himself; the

Lenna Geronimo, daughter of Geronimo, wearing puberty dress. (Courtesy of Smithsonian Institution, National Anthropological Archives, negative no. 2498)

little coyotes just got burned.[61] Remembering that myths teach, the lessons learned by coyote in this little tale can be applied to various situations in marriages, such as when one partner tricks another, or when other possibilities look brighter . . . but really are not.

One of the major purposes of an Apache marriage was to produce children, and if a couple was childless, it was thought the husband might have been bewitched, or perhaps tricked into impotence by a human version of a coyote. On the other hand, a wife's sterility was sometimes attributed to "malice on the part of her mother" or adverse circumstances that occurred during her puberty ceremony.[62] In these and other cases, Apache medicine men and medicine women had rituals to alleviate or eliminate these conditions and thus facilitate pregnancy.

James Haley described an Apache woman's pregnancy as being a time of "equanimity, of care without dread, work without exertion, and receiving special attention without becoming spoiled."[63] It is obvious that he was portraying pregnancy during ideal times; that is, when she was not in peril from any external conditions and could observe certain customs surrounding pregnancy: she didn't ride horses, didn't lift heavy objects, didn't do anything that could shock the fetus. She didn't eat fatty meat, piñon nuts, or intestine; she didn't witness ceremonies at which the *Gah'e* danced because the sight of them might scare the baby. She didn't argue with outsiders because she wasn't certain who was a witch and who wasn't, and the baby could be hexed if she quarreled with a witch. During the dangerous times in an Apache woman's life, she conformed to the conditions around her as best she could while still respecting tradition throughout the duration of her pregnancy, including laboring and giving birth in the customary Apache way.

In olden days the expectant mother wore a maternity belt made of the skins of white-tailed and black-tailed deer, mountain lion, and antelope. These were the animals known to give birth without difficulty, and it was believed that if the mother-to-be wore this belt for a few days only, she would imitate the animals and have an easy birth.

When a Western Apache woman was in labor, she might be "tied to a tree with her hands above her head and legs spread."[64] After the birth occurred, the midwife in attendance (if possible) washed the baby with her own saliva mixed with warm water. Squirting this mixture over the newborn was believed to be very beneficial because of the natural medicinal properties it contained. After the short washing ceremony, the infant was dried with grass, soft moss, or a cloth. Sacred pollen was sprinkled over the newborn and the baby was placed in a cradleboard made by the mother, grandmother, or a female relative.

All Apache births, like those in other cultures, might not have been occasions for joy, however. Certain situations required sometimes harsh actions. Mails reported that "the Apache formerly killed feeble children at birth and that the 'cry babies' were also strangled."[65] Haley wrote about the "dreaded birth of twins." Two babies indicated sexual promiscuity on the part of the wife or a sign of serious spiritual disharmony. "One of the babies was usually destroyed at birth. If one was a boy and the other a girl, the boy was kept."[66] It is difficult to know whether or not the reports recorded by these writers are absolutely accurate. The Apache people needed children and treated them well, recognizing that the future depended in part on procreation. Killing children seems, to this author, to be an extreme action and one not likely to be compatible with the overall intents and purposes of the Apache culture.

Other actions surrounding childbirth, such as disposing of the afterbirth, were carried out in a prescribed, traditional manner. Chiricahua women wrapped the placenta in a piece of cloth or a blanket and placed it in the branches of a nearby fruit-bearing bush or tree. Before the bundle was placed, the midwife blessed it with a special prayer: "May the child live and grow up to see you bear fruit many times." The location of birth remained forever sacred, and the parents and child might return there many times in the child's life.[67]

Other cultural traditions recommended that a nursing mother eat a soup especially prepared for her containing boiled bones, which were beneficial to the production of milk in her breasts. Apache babies were removed from their cradleboards to be nursed, but once their bellies were full and they grew sleepy, they were immediately returned to the carrier, which contained a

> soft bedding of shredded bark or crumpled grass. . . . Over this bedding was laid the tanned, spotted hide of a fawn, the hair side up, or

at times the skins of cottontail rabbits. The baby was then placed on this and between its legs for a diaper was put soft, shredded bark. Another fawn skin, hair side in, was laid over it, the edges tucked in about the baby's body and up under its feet. It was then laced into the carrier with a strip of buckskin.[68]

Occasionally, small items were hung from the top of the cradleboard to aid in the development of the infant's eyes. These could be feathers, pinecones, a squirrel's tail, arrowheads, beads of all sorts, and any talisman that assured good health and a long life for the child. Infants remained in cradleboards until they were approximately six or seven months old, when they were allowed to crawl on the ground, under adult supervision. First haircuts were given to youngsters in the spring of the year they needed them, with a medicine man or medicine woman customarily in attendance for this important occasion. Locks of the hair would be buried under fruit trees to ensure a full head of hair. Moccasins were usually placed on an infant's feet before the second birthday, also under the watchful eye of a medicine man or medicine woman who sang sacred songs during this and other traditional childhood ceremonies.

Terrell commented on the Apache parents' attitude toward their children: "They displayed profound affection for their children but, being realists, they were unsparing in training their sons and daughters to counter and overcome the vicissitudes which they understood would surely confront them."[69] Knowing the hardships their children would face, the parents of Warm Springs Apache chief Victorio and his sister, Lozen, trained their youngsters well. Victorio was one of the most able Indian chiefs in American history, and Lozen was a most skillful Apache warrior; she accompanied the men on their raids and participated in war parties as an equal. She was also, some say, an outstanding medicine woman who had the ability to detect the direction in which the enemy was located. Because of her superb power she eluded capture until the very last, when she surrendered voluntarily with Geronimo's band—the last group of free Apaches.[70]

Apache
Women
Warriors

2

Once the scouts shouted to the squaws to come out and surrender, that they would not be hurt. Derision greeted them. . . . Later, a woman screaming imprecations at them, cried that if Victorio died, "they would eat him, so that no white man should see his body."[1]

The woman threatening to eat the flesh of the respected chief of the Warm Springs Apache band is not named, but few familiar with Apache history would doubt that it was Lozen, Chief Victorio's sister. In her own right a fearsome warrior during the days of freedom, it is entirely possible that Lozen wouldn't hesitate to cannibalize her brother rather than surrender him to an enemy, and commit the violent act with as much facility as the circumstances permitted.

Lozen was an exceptional Apache woman, and one who had the respect of her people because of her abilities and accomplishments. Unlike Lozen, most Apache women did not actively seek confrontations, for it was the custom at the time that most of the wives, sisters, daughters, and other women remained at the stronghold to pray for their men. Also, they were expected to exercise great caution in their behavior. By so doing, it was believed, they could keep bad luck from finding their loved ones.

Occasionally, some women accompanied the warriors as members of a raiding party or a war party. These women's primary duties were cooking, cleaning, and nursing the wounded, even though many women had been trained to run, ride, and shoot when they were youngsters. Donald Cole reported that

> girls in the 11 to 12 age group were given a great deal of physical activity . . . [and] participated in races, both on foot and on horseback, against boys of their same age. Girls and young women were expected to guard the camp and repel attackers in the absence of males. They were also expected to learn to hunt small game. Women, therefore, were trained in the use of rifle, knife, throwing stick, and bow. Necessity then called for the training of girls in at least the minimal combat and survival techniques to make survival probable. Girls were thus instructed in the use of knife, bow, and rifle as well as in escape and evasion, use of camouflage, and handling of horses. . . . Men often taught their wives the use of weapons. On rare occasions, whole classes of girls would be trained in combat along with similar age groups of boys. Initial training included running and such toughening exercises as rolling the snow and pushing snowballs uphill. Use of sling, bow, rifle, and knife followed as young people reached the ages of 8 to 12. Wrestling was a part of the boys' training, but was not usual for girls.[2]

Michael Darrow, the Fort Sill Apache tribal historian says,

> The qualifications, like being able to shoot a gun, ride a horse and run far and fast and the other miscellaneous qualities that would apply to the male warriors were the same for women. The training

process was such that essentially everybody had the same training but with different emphasis. Everybody was supposed to know how to do everything, whether they do it or not. So, the men would need to know how to cook and sew because there might be an occasion when they would need to do that. Women would need to know how to ride horses and follow tracks. Some women would be particularly skilled at things like following tracks or shooting or running. They wouldn't be discouraged from doing it, but they wouldn't necessarily be encouraged.[3]

It has been suggested that women who rode with the men also provided sexual pleasures to the warriors, but this conjecture has never been substantiated.[4]

Authors and researchers have identified at least four Apache women—Dahteste, Gouyen, Siki, and Ishton—who, along with Lozen, were as courageous, daring, and skillful as the men.[5]

Dahteste indeed battled bravely beside her first husband, Apache warrior Anandia, while traveling with Geronimo's band. Her leader called upon her for other duties, however, and Dahteste became the messenger, an important job in the group. Only trusted members were messengers, for if information wasn't delivered or passed on accurately, many lives could be lost—Apache lives. Together with Lozen, Dahteste was responsible for initiating the negotiations with the U.S. Army that led to Geronimo's final surrender in 1886.

Dahteste was imprisoned with others in the band, but her name does not appear on the communications about Geronimo's group sent from the Southwest to Washington. In a telegram dated October 11, 1886, the department commander, a man by the name of Stanley, sent the following message, full of misspellings of Apache names, from San Antonio, Texas, to the adjutant general in Washington:

> Your dispatch of this date received. The following is a list of Apache Indian prisoners under my charge with names, ages, and condition as to marriage, viz: Geronimo, about forty-seven, and wife about thirty-five; Natchez, about thirty-five and wife, about seventeen; Perico, first cousin of Geronimo, about thirty-seven, and wife, about

twenty-eight; Fun, first cousin of Geronimo, about twenty, and wife, about nineteen; Ahwandia, about twenty-six and wife, about twenty-one; Napi, about forty-five and wife, about thirty-five; Yah-nozha, about thirty-two and wife, about twenty; Fishnolthtonz, about twenty-two and wife, about fourteen; Bishi, about forty and wife, about thirty-five; Chapo, about twenty-two and wife about sixteen; Lazaiyah, brother of Napi, about forty-six and wife, about thirty-seven; Motsos, about thirty-five, unmarried; Kilthdigai, about thirty-five, unmarried; Zhonne, about twenty, unmarried; Lonah, about nineteen, unmarried.

Children: Three boys, Skayocarne, twelve years; Gardiltha, ten years; Estchinaeintonyah, seven years; and three girls, Leosanni, six years, parents in San Augustine; Napi's infant, two years; Chapo's baby, one month. Chapo is Geronimo's son.

The conduct of these Indians since they have been here has been excellent. I can learn nothing of their character. George, interpreter, says he knows of character of few only, and that their character is good. The Indians will not inform on each other. With these Indians are two enlisted scouts—Keyehtah, about thirty-eight; Martine, about twenty-seven. Character of both good. Wives of both in Florida.[6]

"Ahwandia"'s wife, a woman of about twenty-one, most likely was Dahteste. It is not unusual that she was unnamed in the telegram, given the perspective of the day about women. But one wonders why the warrior woman Lozen was not mentioned by name and/or marital status. It is virtually certain that the army knew of her exploits and acknowledged that she was indeed a worthy foe, but only the names of the male warriors, single or married, are noted. No unmarried females are mentioned.

Another telegram, sent on October 20, 1886, repeats the names of the male prisoners and adds,

These Indians have been guilty of the worst crimes known to the law, committed under circumstances of great atrocity, and the public safety requires that they be removed far from the scene of their depredations and guarded with the strictest vigilance.[7]

Dahteste had survived the many battles and the physical ailments such as tuberculosis and pneumonia that plagued the Apache people. She married scout Kuni, later called Coonie, after she and Anandia were divorced in the "Indian way." Records don't reveal who left whom, but it didn't take too long for her to find Kuni. "Coonie was a widower with three children. In addition to them, the couple cared for a nephew of Coonie" and two other orphaned children.[8] Dahteste was part of the Apache group that was transferred to Fort Sill in 1894, and she lived on the Oklahoma military post until all the Chiricahuas were released in 1913 to make their homes at Whitetail on the Mescalero Apache Reservation. There, Dahteste and Coonie lived in a tent until their home was built.

Eve Ball wrote about her first meeting with Dahteste, which occurred when the Apache woman was about eighty-nine years old; Mescalero Apache tribal census rolls record Dahteste's birth year as 1860.

It was in 1949 at Mescalero that I met Tah-des-te [an alternate spelling]. Little did I suspect that the frail, white-haired woman was one of the greatest of Apache heroines.

One bitterly cold day in January her step-daughter, Eliza Coonie, brought her to my home. When I answered the door I recognized Eliza and invited the half-frozen women to enter. Wrapped in thin shawls, both were shaking. Eliza's fingers were stiff with cold. I hesitated to take them to a seat before the fireplace but Eliza made the decision to go there. She asked for cold water for her hands. I found that the older woman, too, needed it.

They had driven from Whitetail, Eliza explained, in an open pickup—one with no glass or curtains—and Tah-des-te, her step-mother, was ill. When I got Eliza to lie down, and had wrapped a blanket around the older woman, I made coffee.

Tah-des-te took a cup. Then with her fingers she touched first her stomach and then her eyes. Eliza explained that she was telling me that she was sick, in each.

When Tah-des-te slept I asked Eliza if they would spend the night. I dreaded their long hazardous trip home. Snow was drifting; the road was not paved; they might get stuck in a drift.

No. Hugh, her brother, would be worried. They must go, and soon, for dark comes early in mid-winter.

I hastily assembled a heavy blanket for their laps and gloves for Eliza. Then I thought of an old seal cape, my mother's. It had not been used since her death years before. I'd considered having it remodeled—but nobody wore seal at that time. It wasn't in style.

I wrapped it about Tah-des-te before leaving the house with them to go to the pickup. I had provided Eliza with a worn but heavy short coat, and felt that both were somewhat protected from the blizzard.

After Eliza succeeded in getting the engine running, she asked, "Where did you get the cape?"

"It was my mother's."

"Where is she now?" she asked.

"She died many years ago," I replied.

Eliza reached for the cape, pulled it from around Tah-des-te, threw it at my feet, and drove into the drifting snow!

I realized more keenly than ever that I had much to learn about Apaches.

As I anticipated, it was a long time before Eliza returned with Tah-des-te. After Hugh, her brother, began taking care of my grounds, occasionally the women of the family would stop to pick him up for the return to White Tail.

Hugh had explained to me the taboo against the use of anything that had belonged to the dead; and Eliza accepted my apology.[9]

Elbys Hugar, great-granddaughter of Cochise and now curator of the Mescalero Apache Cultural Center, pointed to a photograph of Dahteste hanging in that museum. "I remember her," said Mrs. Hugar.

When I was very young, she was a very old woman. I used to see her around the reservation. She lived at Whitetail with her niece, Eliza Coonie, and she rode around in a pickup truck that Eliza drove. An old pickup truck. Eliza drove Dahteste and sometimes another woman, Charlotte Goody, into town to do some shopping. They went to Ruidoso or Tularosa. Eliza would help those ladies get what they needed, especially when Dahteste grew old. Dahteste was always dressed nicely in her Apache clothing. She wore beautiful beads, turquoise sometimes, and a very pretty belt. I always admired her beaded bags. She wore her hair straight. Just brushed it out. I don't think I ever saw her braid her hair. She was a nice looking woman, very nice looking.

Dahteste owned a lot of sheep and hired a Mexican man as sheep-herder. . . . She was a Christian woman and went to the Reformed church at Whitetail.

She never had a husband that I know of back then. She and Eliza took part in the activities at the church and also Eliza participated when we had a picnic and contests at the Whitetail day school to celebrate the end of the school year each May. We had all kinds of contests and Eliza Coonie used to win the ladies' races. Eliza outran all the women. She was good at baseball too and played in all the games at Whitetail. She was a tall, thin lady. A quiet person who had respect. Dahteste died of old age. Eliza Coonie died many years ago too.[10]

Today, the roof on Dahteste's house at Whitetail has collapsed inward and the planks cover the floor, itself shaky and warped with age. Outside the dwelling, however, the T-bars of a clothesline, with rust so thick one can scrape it off with a fingernail, still stand a short distance away from what once was a door into the house. Barbed wire is everywhere on her land, lying flat on the ground, or waving precipitously as it dangles from tree stumps used as fence posts. A metal water trough, once filled with water to quench the thirst of animals, now contains household debris: broken dishes, odd shoes, ropes, an old belt, rags, pieces of wood, and a gear from a truck. Rotting wood and boards with rusty nails exposed lie on the land, decaying. That old pickup truck, long ago useless, is now sinking into the soft soil and becoming covered with mountain grasses. A garter snake slithers out from under a rusty red fender, probably annoyed at being disturbed, and crawls across the field toward a now-overgrown road that passes in front of Dahteste's house.

Elbys Hugar also knew Siki Toklanni, a woman who was with

Siki Toclanni (or Toklanni), circa 1898.
(Courtesy of Fort Sill Museum, Fort Sill, Oklahoma, photo no. P3605)

Geronimo's band when the group surrendered in 1886. Long before this final event, however, Siki had an incredible personal history. Born in 1866 (according to Mescalero Apache tribal census rolls) and the daughter of Chief Loco, a well-respected Apache leader, Siki had been at Tres Castillos with Chief Victorio and his group when Mexican soldiers either killed or took captive all the members of his group. Five women, including Siki, were sent to Mexico City and sold as slaves to the owner of a nearby hacienda. For three years they waited for an opportunity to sneak off, and finally they did, starting a journey of more than one thousand miles on foot to return to their Apache people. Carrying only one knife and one blanket, they made their way back home—an astounding feat. This flight to safety has been described in great detail by Apache historian Eve Ball.[11]

Perhaps it was Siki's puberty ceremony that gave her the stamina and courage she needed. Warm Springs Apache James Kaywaykla, also a survivor of the massacre at Tres Castillos, remembered Siki's ceremonial costume.

> It consisted of long beaded buckskin moccasins, an upper garment, and a two-piece skirt, trimmed in long fringe cut from the skin, with beads and hundreds of tiny cone-shaped tin jingles. Each jingle had a string of skin drawn through it and knotted to prevent its loss, leaving an inch-long strip to sew to the skirt. I think I chewed sinew all that winter to soften it for use in sewing.
>
> The upper garment was made of a long piece of the leather with a slit cut crosswise for the head, and the ends hanging in front and back. Fringe fifteen inches long covered the arms and hung in graceful rows along both sides of the garment. Siki wore two eagle plumes floating from her long hair, and many silver and turquoise ornaments which I did not remember having seen. They had been carried in the folds of Grandmother's moccasins.[12]

Mrs. Hugar still recalls Siki.

> I used to see Siki and her husband Toklanni when I went with my parents down the road. On the side of the hill they played cards, *kunkan* mostly. They used to play cards out in the open. Some people still play there today, and once in a while I take part. It's a very enjoyable game. We go to Juarez, Mexico, and buy the cards. You play with two decks at a time. Siki and her husband had a daughter that I remember. Emma. She got married to a man named Rufus, and I think they had two daughters. Flora and Frieda. Frieda is the oldest.

They all used to live at Whitetail. Emma's husband, Rufus, worked with the cowboys, and sometimes with the Apache Red Hat crew. They fight fires. I remember them when they lived up there at White-tail. Siki was a very nice lady. She spoke the Chiricahua language in a tone of voice that made you want to hear more and more. All of the people who lived at Whitetail are gone today. It's just like a ghost town up there. Some of the old shacks are still up, though, and the old schoolhouse is still standing. The church is no longer there; it was moved to the Elk area. Elk is another small community. Somebody is probably living in the church right now.

But the cemetery is up there at Whitetail. The Istees (Victorio's descendants) and the Kazhes and some other Chiricahuas are buried there. No one is in charge of the cemetery, but the relatives of the people go back up there and fix the fence and take care of the graves. The cemetery is associated with the Reformed church and most of the people buried there were from the church.[13]

Another notable Apache woman, Gouyen (Siki Toklanni's aunt), began her battle experiences when she was a young woman with two children, and also part of Chief Victorio's Warm Springs Apache band. After a particularly arduous foray into Mexico, the group of Apaches rested at Tres Castillos in northern Mexico. Unexpectedly, armed Mexicans attacked, killing seventy-eight Apaches; sixty-eight women and children were captured to be sold into slavery (a favorite Mexican means of disposing of prisoners of war), and the livestock taken totaled 120 horses, 38 mules, and 12 burros. Only seventeen Apaches escaped the slaughter, two of whom were Gouyen and her four-year-old son, Kaywaykla. A baby daughter was killed. Gouyen's husband at that time was elsewhere, but he also died soon afterward, brutally killed and mutilated during a Comanche raid on another Apache group that Gouyen and her family had joined for safety after the Tres Castillos assault.

A legendary tale is told about the revenge of Gouyen (a name that means "wise woman") upon the death of her husband. She donned her puberty ceremony buckskin dress and walked away from camp in the darkness one night, carrying a water jug and dried meat stored in a pouch at her waist.

Her plan was to find the Comanche camp and the warrior who had scalped and killed her husband. For three nights she followed the trail, and on the fourth she discovered their camp. They were celebrating, and bonfires blazed with the heat of the Comanche victory over the Apaches. Gouyen's husband's scalp was owned by the chief. She saw it in his possession.

First, Gouyen stole a horse and tied it some distance from the half-drunken group. Then she returned and slipped into a circle of dancers. Making her way seductively toward the chief, she flirted with him and lured him into the shadows away from the others. After a brief and bloody struggle, Gouyen killed the chief with his own knife. Then, holding the weapon steady, she scalped him, cut his beaded breechclout away from his body, and tore the moccasins off his feet. Afterward, she galloped the stallion for two days back to her camp, where she collapsed in the arms of her dead husband's parents, her puberty dress stained and smeared with the chief's dried blood. When she revived, she presented her in-laws with the Comanche leader's scalp, his clothing, and his footwear.

Gouyen eventually married again, the second time to Apache warrior Ka-ya-ten-nae, and they reared her surviving child, Kaywaykla. The family later was taken prisoner by the U.S. Army and held at Fort Sill. Gouyen's grave is in the Apache cemetery at Fort Sill in a shady glen filled with the graves of the Kaywaykla family, including her son, who was given the name James. While he was a prisoner, the boy James Kaywaykla attended school with other Apache children in Carlisle, Pennsylvania. He married Dorothy Naiche, daughter of Chiricahua chief Naiche and Eh-clah-eh. After they were released from prison, Dorothy and James Kaywaykla made their home in Apache, Oklahoma. The Fort Sill Apache Tribal Complex is today built on property that once belonged to the Kaywaykla family. In later years James Kaywaykla collaborated with Eve Ball in producing a book, *In the Days of Victorio*, that has been hailed as a classic in literature about the Apache people.

Many other Apache women, including Geronimo's sister Ishton, didn't live long enough to become prisoners of war. Ishton and a young daughter were killed in a cavalry attack, but her husband and son, Chief Juh and Asa Daklugie, survived. They were two of the most valiant Apache leaders.

Juh met Ishton when they were both quite young, long before the hos-

Gouyen, her son Kaywaykla, and her second husband, Kaytennae.
(Ben Wittick, photographer. Courtesy of Special Collections, General Library,
University of New Mexico, negative no. 989-022-0001)

tilities took their toll. Juh's family and others of the Nednhi Apache band, traveling north from their home in Mexico, would visit the Bedonkohe Apaches in the area that is now Arizona and New Mexico. Two Bedonkohe children, Geronimo and his favorite sister, Ishton, played with Juh and his friends in typical fashion: the boys taunted the girls and stole baskets of acorns from them. Ishton grew into a tall, beautiful woman who had slaves of her own and wore gorgeous beaded buckskin robes. She married Juh, and their son, Daklugie, later recalled that when she was not actively participating in an expedition, Ishton directed the victory feast.[14] It was shrewd and influential Ishton who suggested much of the Nednhi warriors' strategy, according to Daklugie, but she did it indirectly and let Juh take the credit for successful campaigns against their enemies.

In contrast, Victorio's sister, Lozen, was always directly involved and highly visible—to her people, to their enemies, and to the spirit world. Lozen is remembered as a powerful medicine woman. Visualize her silhouette framed by the fiery setting sun as she stands on a mesa with outstretched hands raised high. Lifting her face and voice to the blazing sky, Lozen sings:

> Upon the earth
> On which we live
> USSEN has Power.
> This Power he grants me
> For locating the enemy.
> I search for that enemy
> Which only USSEN, Creator of Life
> Can reveal to me.[15]

Moving slowly in a clockwise direction, Lozen halted when a tingling feeling or change in the color of her palms became noticeable. The direction she faced when she stopped was usually the place where the enemy was located. This "medicine power" enabled each band she accompanied to avoid capture, to the delight of the Apaches and the chagrin of the Mexican and American armies. Occasionally, the sensation became so intense that her palms turned purple, meaning the enemy was very near. The farther away the foe, the weaker was her physical reaction.

To the Warm Springs Apache band into which she was born in the late 1840s, and to the groups she later joined, Lozen was prophet, warrior, and medicine woman. "I depend on Lozen," said Victorio. "She is skillful in dressing wounds; when I got a bullet through my shoulder, she burned the thorns from a leaf of nopal, split it, and bound the fleshy side to the wound. The next day I rode."[16]

Historians have speculated about whether or not Victorio's death in 1880 under siege from the Mexican army at Tres Castillos would have occurred if Lozen had been with them. Had she not been away from her band on a raid, she might have used her powers that fateful October day and warned the group well in advance. Regardless of what might have been, however, Lozen continued her warrior's way without interruption following her brother's death. Riding with the new chief, Nana, Lozen and others immediately took their obligatory revenge according to Apache custom.

One author has described the circumstances surrounding that tumultuous time in American and Mexican history as being one in which

> the Indians had a number of advantages. Whenever their horses wore out, they changed them—their remount depots being the nearest ranches or settlements. They carried practically nothing but their arms and ammunition. Their commissary was the country—the mescal, the mesquite bean, and the prickly pear. For meat they occasionally shot a deer, but the usual repast was a horse or mule, slaughtered when it could run no longer, and cut up almost before life was extinct, to be roasted and gorged by the warriors. The Apaches knew every spot where water could be found, no matter how small and inaccessible. But they did not need water like the white man. With a pebble under the tongue to keep the saliva flowing, one of Nana's raiders could go without water under the blaze of the desert sun two days longer than a white man could survive. . . . In less than two months, Nana, handicapped by age and physical disabilities, led his handful of braves over a thousand miles of enemy territory, maintaining himself and his followers in the country as they went. He

fought eight battles with the Americans, winning them all; killed anywhere from thirty to fifty of his enemy, wounded large numbers more; captured two women and not less than two hundred horses and mules; eluded pursuit by more than a thousand soldiers, not to mention three or four hundred civilians—and did it all with a force which numbered only fifteen warriors at the start and never exceeded forty braves.[17]

Lozen, of course, was an essential part of the raids as she took vengeance for her brother's murder. She eventually joined forces with Geronimo's band and rode with him until the last. With Dahteste, Lozen was responsible for the early negotiations prior to the final surrender in 1886. She was photographed while the Apaches were in transit from Arizona to their first prison camp at Fort Marion, Florida. It is the only known photo of this Apache woman warrior who defied all known attempts to capture her, and whose medicine helped keep her people free.

During the period of U.S. history between 1860 and 1886, a time when Lozen, Geronimo, Naiche, and other Apaches were riding, the American government was conducting an extensive "roundup" of the Indian peoples. Official policy regarding Native Americans was made in Washington, D.C., by elected officials who had almost no understanding of any of the tribes, much less their customs. Many of these policies mandated that the "savages" be put on reservations where their activities could be controlled by civilian and military agents. Death or incarceration in a prisoner-of-war camp were the only alternatives for any who dared resist the plan.

Apaches trying to avoid capture and subsequent imprisonment often crossed the border into northern Mexico, where they stole fresh horses and killed livestock for food. In desperation, after its own troops were unable to subdue the invaders, the Mexican government hired civilian bounty hunters to help the soldiers. These mercenaries were not particular whose scalp they delivered for a few pesos, as long as there was black hair attached. Since most of the Mexican people were also dark, the situation rapidly deteriorated; the mercenaries were killing Mexican citizens, calling

Apache prisoners: Geronimo and Naiche, front row, third and fourth from right; Lozen, top row, third from right; Ha-o-zinne (Naiche's wife), top row, center. (Courtesy of Smithsonian Institution, National Anthropological Archives, negative no. 2517-A)

them Indians, and taking their scalps to Mexican authorities, who were paying them per head. Of course, the Apaches were being blamed for the murders.

On the other hand, the Apaches needed to eliminate the people chasing them. One favorite technique was to shoot the horses out from under the Mexican or American riders. After that, it didn't take long at all for the Apaches to put an end to the soldiers or civilians frantically scurrying on foot for their lives.

> They say they used to tie Mexicans with their hands behind their backs. Then they turned the women loose with axes and knives to kill the Mexican prisoners. The man could hardly run and the women would chase him around until they killed him. . . . When a brave warrior is killed, the men go out for about three Mexicans. They bring them back for the women to kill in revenge. The women ride at them on horseback, armed with spears.[18]

In 1871 the Arizona Territorial Legislature authorized publication of almost a hundred sworn testimonies attesting to incredible hostilities by the Apaches. Governor A. P. K. Safford was one of the respondents quoted in the volume. He said he didn't consider "any portion [of Arizona] safe from depredations by the Apaches. . . . Scarcely a day passes without murders and robberies . . . the [Apaches] are cruel in the extreme." He personally had seen "the charred remains of a white man who had evidently been burned alive."[19] Death by fire was a technique used frequently by the Apaches. They would hang their captured enemy head down from a tree or any other available brace and then build a fire under the victim's head. Unable to move, the individual suffered death by immolation in a slow, agonizing manner. Another favorite method of punishment was said to be staking an enemy to the ground over an anthill and allowing the ants to slowly torture him to death.

Naturally, as a warrior, Lozen participated in these actions, riding confidently into any battle and ensuring that she got her fair share of the kills. Lozen was invited to councils. Said old Apache Charlie Smith in an interview, "To us she was as a Holy Woman and she was regarded and treated as such. White Painted Woman herself was not more respected."[20]

For years before he died, Lozen's brother Chief Victorio had tried to negotiate a separate peace with the U.S. Army on behalf of the Warm Springs band. His people wanted to live in southwestern New Mexico, on a reservation of their own, surrounded by the familiar hills and valleys they loved best of all. That was their homeland, Victorio told the American army officers, and if the government would assign the Warm Springs people to that area, he promised they would cause no more trouble. Instead, instructions came from Washington, D.C., to round up the Apaches and move them to San Carlos, a barren and hot desert site in southern Arizona. There they had to mingle and live with hundreds of other Indians, some of whom had been their enemies. Recurring friction among the unhappy bands was aggravated further by constant feuding between the civilian and military personnel in charge of the reservation. Finally, in 1880, more than three hundred frustrated Warm Springs Apaches, including Lozen, took matters into their own hands and literally stampeded their way out of San Carlos. After stealing army horses, one of Lozen's favorite pastimes,[21] they headed east, free to be themselves for a while before the government rounded them up again. Until then, however, they could live as they pleased and ride with the wind across the land they loved so dearly.

Lozen was able to ride with the men and take care of the women and children because she was unmarried, an unusual situation for an Apache woman.[22] Legend says she carried a vision in her heart of a special warrior, one whom no mortal could rival or equal, and so she remained alone. When Lozen was about sixteen years old, Apache folklore tells, she saw and met what came to be called the Gray Ghost. Stories describe this warrior as being very handsome and having great power, riding alone on a magnificent stallion in the arroyos and on the mesas throughout Apacheland. The Gray Ghost, during one of his many rides, actually came into a Warm Springs camp and spent time with the people. He told their leader, Victorio, that he too was a chief, but from other lands far away toward the east. A wagon passed nearby as they were talking. It was guarded by twelve men who were neither Indian, nor Mexican, nor American. Inside the wagon sat a beautiful young woman attended by a wrinkled old hag. As the wagon continued westward, the handsome chief rode his steed after it and was never seen again by the Warm Springs people. However,

Lozen remembered him fondly, and despite her close associations with many brave Apache warriors, she never found one appealing enough to overcome her memory of the Gray Ghost of her youth.

It is possible that Lozen met a member of the Seneca Tribe who was exploring the Southwest in search of a new location for his New York tribe. In the late 1850s and early 1860s the federal government was attempting to relocate the Seneca onto reservations in Kansas or beyond.

After the rider moved on, Lozen gave no sign of discontent with regard to either her marital status or the dual roles she fulfilled, one as a warrior and one safeguarding the women and children. As a fighter, Lozen gladly followed any instructions given her by the chief, but if it was the chief's wish that she stay away from the hostile actions and help the more dependent members of the band, she willingly did so. It was no secret, however, that she preferred being in the thick of a good battle.

Kaywaykla described an episode that illustrates Lozen's prowess.

> When the guard left the horses and started toward the fire, she must make an attempt to secure [a horse]. Already she had selected a powerful steed, one of the most restless. When the guard had passed the fire, she would tie her leather rope around its lower jaw, cut the hobbles, and ride. She crept softly to the animal and quickly tied the rope. . . . She leaped to its back and turned it toward the river. Bullets whizzed past her head as the horse slid down the bank and plunged into the river.[23]

Lozen's unique powers, including her ability to steal horses with such ease, are believed to have begun back in the days of her puberty ceremony. At that time, custom required a young woman to go into the mountains for four days, keep a constant vigil, and return to the tribe after having been visited by whatever animal or spirit would give her "power" for the rest of her life. Lozen's power to discern the direction of the enemy was indeed a rare example of a special visitation.

Ironically, at the end of her freedom there was no need for Lozen to use either her superior fighting skills or her medicine. As a member of Geronimo's band in 1886, she was well aware of the hopeless alternatives offered the less than fifty Apaches who were still free. They had evaded five thousand U.S. Army officers and soldiers for years, but could no longer prevail. The possibility of starvation or death was all that was left if they remained free. Some of Geronimo's warriors at first refused to listen to his talk about surrender. Others, those weary of constantly fighting enormous odds to stay alive, were eager to be with their wives and children already imprisoned in Florida. After carefully considering the circumstances and the warriors' various points of view, Geronimo sent Lozen and Dahteste to arrange a meeting with the Americans. Long negotiations, promises, and compromises led to a peaceful surrender, a decision Geronimo regretted for the rest of his life.

At about the same time (September 1886), four hundred Apaches from Fort Apache and the San Carlos Reservation in Arizona were also sent by train to Pensacola and St. Augustine, Florida.[24] Less than one year later, at 1:00 A.M. on April 27, 1887, the government shipped the Apaches from Florida to Mount Vernon Barracks, north of Mobile, Alabama. Eugene Chihuahua, son of Chief Chihuahua, recalled,

> We were to be stationed at an old army fort near Mobile. It was on the west side of the Mobile River, and about twenty-five miles or so from the Gulf of Mexico. It had been built of brick in the 1830s and had been abandoned. We thought anything would be better than Fort Marion with its rain, mosquitoes and malaria, but we were to find out that it was good in comparison with Mt. Vernon Barracks. We didn't know what misery was till they dumped us in those swamps. There was no place to climb to pray. If we wanted to see the sky, we had to climb a tall pine.[25]

Married couples lived together at Mount Vernon in shacks with dirt floors; unmarried men were housed together. It rained most of the time, the roofs leaked, and Apache babies died from mosquito bites. Forced into yet another unfamiliar environment, many adults and children became very ill, victims of sicknesses and diseases against which they had no natural immunity. Simple colds developed quickly into pneumonia, exacerbated by the year-round wet weather; mosquitos, breeding by the hundreds of thousands in stagnant water near the prison camps, caused malaria; infections spread rapidly, causing many to die each day; dreaded smallpox

Captive Apaches at Fort Bowie.
(Courtesy of Western History Collections, University of Oklahoma Library,
photograph no. 873)

was especially virulent in the camp and became a most devastating killer
of Apaches. "The danger of contagious disease attacking the Indians and
spreading is, in my opinion, a matter worthy of prompt and serious consideration," wrote Herbert Welsh in a report dated April 1887. "The rations
are insufficient," he continued, "and the clothing of the Indians during the
winter has been totally insufficient and unsuitable. Most of them wore only
the rags which they brought with them from Arizona."[26] His reference
was to the clothes the Apache prisoners hadn't taken off for six months
because the U.S. Army hadn't issued them any others.

The proud and once-free Apache people were at long last under the control of the U.S. government and were hungry, sick, and dying in captivity.
John Turcheneske, a researcher, reported that

> by 1894, the damp climate first encountered in Florida and subse-
> quently in Alabama, by a people accustomed to Arizona's dry moun-
> tain air, decimated Chiricahua ranks by nearly half. This situation,

as well as a desire to make these Indians economically independent, prompted the military to remove them to Fort Sill, Oklahoma.[27]

Fort Sill was a military reservation that had been set apart as an Indian reservation for the use and benefit of the Wichita, Kiowa, and Comanche Indians. To accommodate the Apaches, a tract of 26,987 acres was added to that parcel of land, then two smaller tracts of 893 and 372 acres were appended. Captain Hugh L. Scott of the Seventh Cavalry was instructed to confer with the Kiowa and Comanche Indians to gain their consent in having the Apache people located near them. They agreed, and the result was the creation of a "permanent status for the Apache Indians in the Fort Sill Reservation, which can only be removed, as it was created, with the consent of the Indians and the approval of Congress."[28]

Lozen never reached Fort Sill. At Mount Vernon she caught the "coughing sickness," as tuberculosis was called.[29] Sadly, her health had also surrendered, and she died in captivity in Alabama, one of six women, one man, and fifteen children who never left Mobile. She was buried in an unmarked grave.

Apache
Women
from
Mescalero

3

THE RESERVATION SETTING

Near the Mescalero Apache Reservation, the U.S. Army routinely tests its weapons on a firing range at White Sands, New Mexico, a barren strip of gypsum and desert growth that has had an important role in American military history. Traffic must halt for an hour or so on the four-lane highway during a "missile alert." Here, deadly weapons have the right-of-way. Trinity Site hides a hundred or so miles to the north; it is opened only twice yearly to public viewing. On those occasions, cars wait in long lines, as if in a funeral procession, to enter the area where an atomic bomb was exploded, thus changing the ways of the world. What visitors see is a fenced-off area, not very large, and not very threatening today. Actually, it is rather disappointing, until one stops to realize that the technology displayed inside the fence could destroy humankind and the planet. Then one is dumbstruck at the enormity of the events that occurred just a few feet away.

The Mescalero Apache Reservation contrasts distinctly with its military neighbor. A tall, green pine oasis established long before the interlopers arrived, Mescalero is life that insists on being seen and heard. Icy water gurgles in streams crisscrossing a land kept soft and cool by winter snows and summer rains. Healthy horses nibble tall grass along the federal route bisecting the reservation, as hawks and crows, mountain blue jays, and other birds call challenges to each other amid the trees. Every five days or thereabouts, eagles fly in to roost in evergreen trees and catch the fish that swim in large, mountain-clean Lake Mescalero. Meantime, ducks float by, squawking and teaching their young the ways of the water, all the while watching the people standing lakeside, watching them. Young and old folks walk beside the main road, and others drive their vehicles to and from reservation destinations. At the hub of the village, tribal administrative offices, a post office, the Mescalero Apache Cultural Center, the tribal store, and a small café occupy space that, for the last century, has held various types of government buildings. Up the road, the Mescalero Reformed Church and St. Joseph's Catholic Church face each other diagonally across the highway, seemingly (but not really) in competition for the souls of the people.

Three groups of Apaches share this place: the Mescalero, whose home this has always been; the Lipan, a small band who are the least-known inhabitants; and the Chiricahua, the most famous Apaches in American history.

Information provided by the tribe and printed on a menu at one of the reservation's popular restaurants, Geronimo's Southwest Deli, declares,

> The Mescalero Apache Reservation long recognized by Spanish, Mexican, and American Treaties was formally established by Executive Order of President Ulysses S. Grant on May 27, 1873. Mescaleros on the reservation numbered about 400 when the reservation was established.[1]

To this group was added the Lipan Apaches, brought north from Chihuahua, Mexico, about 1903, after they had suffered heavy losses in the Texas wars. And in 1913 the Chiricahuas arrived from Fort Sill. All became members of the Mescalero Apache Tribe in 1936, after the tribe was reorganized under the provisions of the federal Indian Organization Act. Today, along with 2,900 inhabitants, the reservation's nearly 500,000 acres contain four sacred mountains—Sierra Blanca, Guadalupe, Three Sisters Mountain, and Oscura Mountain Peak—representing the four directions of the universe. On an economic level, the tribe operates a sawmill, a ski resort, and the celebrated Inn of the Mountain Gods, a lodge

> resting on sacred territorial grounds . . . offering guests the opportunity to experience the richness of a living civilization rooted in centuries past . . . with picturesque tipis gracing the shores . . . with hills of rolling golf greens, the swimming pool, spa and other recreational facilities blending harmoniously with nature in a setting of crystal streams, manicured lawns and brilliant sun rays peaking [sic] through trees and dancing on the sacred resort grounds.[2]

It's all true. Not mentioned, but also an important part of life on the reservation, is Bingo of Mescalero, a several-nights-a-week treat for many Apaches and visitors hoping to make a few dollars or win a fortune. All the players applaud the winners at the end of each game; a nice touch.

Everyone who lives on this reservation is a winner, not in terms of dollars, perhaps, but just by being able to enjoy the glory of the surroundings. One hears in the wind the songs of the Mountain Spirits, those colorful representations of the sacred Apache spirit world. The dancing spirits appear on special occasions such as puberty ceremonies and important gatherings of Apaches, but their image is everywhere, from a fully costumed, larger-than-life carving in the cultural museum to a tiny figure on a tribal license plate. The Mountain Spirit dancers are the tribe's official logo, and so one sees representations of them on correspondence, on the sides of buildings, on bumper stickers, and on packs of wooden matches available at the Inn of the Mountain Gods. Even the advertisement for Bingo of Mescalero shows a Mountain Spirit dancing in the center of a circle.

All Apaches have a personal place in their hearts for these dancers, called by some *ga'n*, or *Gah'e*. They have accompanied the people through untold hardships and humiliation and have been close at hand to enjoy and share in any successes. The dancers are intensely spiritual and connect the Apache people with their origins, and with a world few outsiders are privileged to understand. It is easy to imagine the *Gah'e* waiting in the caves in the Sacramento Mountains for the 183 Chiricahua, newly released from confinement in Fort Sill, Oklahoma, to arrive at the Tularosa, New Mexico, depot after a long train trip from Fort Sill. Among those arriving on April 4, 1913, were

> Geronimo's widow with her young grandnephew Paul Guydelkon and his father . . . Naiche, his wife Ha-o-zinne, and five of his children; his old mother, Dos-teh-seh, daughter of Mangas Coloradas and widow of Cochise; his two half-sisters, daughters of Cochise; and Ha-o-zinne's parents, Beshe and U-go-hun, and her half brother, Calvin Zhonne. The chief left in the Fort Sill cemetery the graves of his wives Nah-de-yole and E-clah-heh and eight of his children; and Dorothy Naiche, the wife of James Kaywaykla, remained in Oklahoma. . . . Tah-das-te [Dahteste] had remarried and went with her husband to Mescalero. . . . Toklanni and Siki with their children. . . . So did Kaahteney, but he had buried Guyan [Gouyen] at Fort Sill.[3]

Mescalero Apaches and others met the former prisoners, who then traveled by horse-drawn wagons to the agency headquarters before a trip to Whitetail, a remote area of the reservation, where they would be permanently settled. "For the Chiricahuas who returned to Mescalero in 1913 and 1914, the Government built small frame houses at Whitetail eighteen miles from the Agency," reported one author.[4] He was correct, but there is much more to the saga. More than one month after their arrival at Mescalero, Major George W. Goode, former officer in charge of the ex-prisoners, returned to Mescalero to check on the progress of the Apaches. He found them still encamped at the agency headquarters and still looking forward to being housed at Whitetail. The wells for drinking water, stock tanks, roads, and houses were not ready, and as more and more time passed, many government and church officials became concerned.

Adding to the delay, the Apaches also became unwitting victims of a political situation, one in which a powerful New Mexico senator, Albert B. Fall, tried to exercise his wish to have the lands at Mescalero turned into a national park. By so doing, the land would not be for Apache use but would be opened for grazing, and it might be possible for the legislator to obtain the mineral rights and royalties.

Meanwhile, most of the Chiricahua were still waiting to reach Whitetail. By October only thirty families were located up there, in a "narrow, eight-mile-long valley over seven thousand feet in elevation which periodically suffered severe winter cold, heavy snowfalls, late and early frosts."[5] All the other families remained at the agency headquarters through that winter of 1913. By January 1914, the Apache Indian agent at Mescalero, Clarence R. Jeffries, was pleading with his Indian Office superiors in Washington for farm machinery, housing appliances, an increase in food rations, and adequate medical facilities. At the same time, Senator Fall, whose original legislation was defeated, reintroduced his measure and Mescalero was once again in danger of becoming a national park. Efforts were simultaneously under way to stock the reservation with cattle, for which Jeffries asked Washington for $200,000. The actual appropriation received much later for livestock was $75,000. In mid-October 1914 a devastating fire ruined most of the oat crop at Whitetail, planted by the first inhabitants, and early snows prevented harvest of the remaining crop. The Chiricahua were destitute.

By spring 1915, housing at Whitetail for all the Chiricahua still had not been completed, and the structures that had been erected were woefully inadequate. Said James O. Arthur, Reformed church missionary, "when the high winds from the west" come "sweeping down the canyon, every crack and knot-hole is discovered to admit the cooling breeze. Homes were built upon wooden posts for a foundation," and constructed "of lumber that went from the standing tree to the carpenters' hands in a month's time, so green that the sap oozed out with every nail driven into it." When these dwellings finally dried out, floors, inside ceilings, and walls became surfeited with cracks such that "the knots drop out of the boards."[6] Jeffries resigned.

A new agent, William A. Light, fared better. He believed in the Indians' right to their reservation and showed economic foresight by building the Apaches' cattle business. At the end of 1917 the herd was worth more than 20 percent over the original purchase price. Improvements at White-tail, under Light's direction, included storage sheds, cisterns, gardens, root cellars, and fencing.

In 1918 a severe drought affected the oat crop once again. Of approximately 608 acres planted, less than 70 acres produced. The people "had very little to live on," said Light.[7] Asa Daklugie and Eugene Chihuahua, two of the leaders, put it more bluntly: "At the present time some of our number are existing upon less than white people feed to their dogs."[8]

On and on it went for several years and several more agents. After ten years the Apaches' livestock business was better subsidized by Washington and Senator Fall's scheme was a thing of the past. But adequate housing at Whitetail continued to be a problem. Two and one-half decades later, things seemed better:

> The Superintendent of this Agency is promoting the most ambitious housing program that has ever been attempted on an Apache reservation. His plan includes the erection of one hundred and fifty new, up-to-date little four room frame houses, with adjoining barn, chicken house, and privy. These cottages are fitted out with neat, substantial furniture—a wood stove for the living room, a good range and sink for the kitchen, and, for other rooms, iron bedsteads and suitable chairs, tables, and dressers. All this furniture is of as good quality as is to be found in the home of the ordinary white man. Some of these houses have already been erected to replace those built for the Chiricahuas twenty-five years ago. . . . When the program shall have been completed every Indian on the reservation will have a sanitary, well-furnished house to live in if he will occupy it; and the encouraging fact is they are actually living in them.[9]

The grand design never happened.

Rev. Robert Schut, pastor of the Mescalero Reformed Church, said regarding Whitetail today,

> Almost nobody lives out there now. I think there's one or two houses . . . ; housing projects came in here, people moved in [toward

the center of the reservation] because of transportation, roads, and that sort of thing. We had a chapel out there and most of those [Chiricahua] who came [to Mescalero] were affiliated with the Reformed church then.[10]

Today, directions to Whitetail are difficult to obtain, as is permission to travel there. The road is unpaved but well maintained with gravel and stone placed smoothly after frequent scrapings. If one follows this road to its end, it leads through Whitetail and out of the vacated settlement to a place known among the Apaches as Number One Cow Camp. Up there, today, Mescalero cowboys take care of the tribe's herd in summer pasture. Among other sights on this winding road, a traveler sees hundreds of cows, bulls, and calves meandering slowly, very slowly, across the road and back again. If an animal feels like stopping in the middle of a driver's route, the driver stops and waits until the livestock decides what to do. They think they own the place. And they do.

In the spring, purple and yellow wildflowers line the sides of the route and an abundance of dandelions colors the gently sloping, wild-grass–covered earth. Very, very tall lodgepole pines and ponderosa pines grow in abundance. On a damp day their aroma is more than refreshing—it's cleansing. After a rain or heavy spring snow, the land remains wet for a long time and the forest cover holds moisture well. It is surprisingly cooler on the road to Whitetail than one might imagine. The hot sun that warms different regions of the Mescalero Apache Reservation takes its time finding a way through the tall evergreens. The air is always crystal clear. No pollutants of any kind invade this unique atmosphere. Road maintenance calls for heavy equipment, but the road needs so little attention that exhaust fumes from the machinery are not a pollution threat. Very few cars or trucks utilize the route, so the consequences of frequent vehicle use are virtually nil. No debris litters the roadside, and the only evidence of human intrusion into this pristine setting is official signs posting speed limits of 25, 30, or 35 miles per hour. Wild turkeys crossing the road do their part to slow vehicles also, whether one stops to admire them or simply stops to let the brood pass. They are a rare sight—two grown birds with about a dozen little ones all around, darting through the brush to some secret place beyond. Or, in the distance, one glimpses several white-tailed deer nervously staring at the interlopers through the safety of the trees. Occasionally, a wild horse, thin almost to the point of starvation, races beside an automobile, ribs heaving while the animal's legs and feet pound the soft ground, driven more by fright than fervor. Most important, however, is the feeling of deep serenity one gets while driving toward Whitetail. There is peace in the forest, and it is not the kind created by human beings. Undoubtedly, each Chiricahua family experienced the same sensation as they made their way up the trail to their new home seven thousand feet above sea level.

If it was a rainy day when they arrived at the settlement, they would have seen gray and black clouds rolling into and among the tall pines, would have heard the close by echo of thunder across the mountains, and may have seen a flash of lightning just behind and above them. It would have been cool, or even cold, and the breezy, moist air would have chilled them to the bone.

A schoolhouse, minus windowpanes but otherwise still intact, and two sturdy houses made of some type of masonry greet visitors today, but at the center of the village when the Chiricahuas people arrived was a small meadow to the right of the road, a soft downward slope in the earth. This is where the oat crop would be planted. Around and above and into the woods beyond the small pastureland, houses (most with two rooms, not four) stretched along the road, ending on the right beside a parcel of land perfect for a horse corral.

"The chairman of the tribe is talking about putting up a monument near the old school to remember the Chiricahuas,"[11] says Elbys Hugar, the great-granddaughter of Cochise, with happiness in her voice. Now there are no commemorative plaques or designations, or any apparent sign that this small abandoned village high in the mountains on the Mescalero Apache Reservation played an important part in American history, but Mrs. Hugar remains optimistic that someday soon Whitetail will be appropriately recognized.

Today, the houses at Whitetail are forsaken, falling to the earth like wounded warriors, dying this time not from bullets but from the changing values of the Apache way. One tall wooden cross, the upright beam made from a peeled pine pole and the crossbar nailed into a chinked square on the pole, marks the spot where an unknown Apache is buried. It towers over the concrete foundation of what was, in times past, probably a very sturdy building. The name of the deceased, once carefully lettered on the crossbar, has, of course, been obliterated by the weather. The longer one stands in respectful silence at the grave, the more apparent it becomes that the anonymity of that lonely, individual burying ground symbolizes all that has happened to Whitetail. Even the barbed wire that once defined various homesites and livestock grazing areas in the village is disappearing, hidden by creeping, crawling natural vegetation that is reclaiming the land. The remains of what must have been dozens of miles of barbed wire used at Whitetail threaten trespassers by waving in the breeze from fence posts tilted drunkenly from decay, by springing up from around the corner of an old barn to snare an unsuspecting ankle, and by hiding under weather-beaten boards rotting on the ground. Whole rolls of rusting barbed wire, never used, are hanging from old tree limbs on liver brown nails hammered into sides of deteriorating barn walls, and lying on the ground too close to that lonely gravesite. After seeing so much of it, one wonders if the barbed wire symbolizes something else; if, perhaps, the abundance of this piercing fence material tests a visitor to Whitetail by challenging her intentions: if she can negotiate around, under, above, and between the barbs without cutting her skin to shreds, she has permission to be there.

In other places at Whitetail, discarded toys, single shoes, a dirty blanket or two, and similar artifacts of days past are strewn around inside dilapidated structures that once were the Apaches' homes. Doors have been flung wide open or are dangling from a broken hinge, just waiting to fall off. In fact, some houses have no doors. They have dropped flat to the ground, exhausted, not far from where they used to hang. Now once-shiny doorknobs are corroded with rust and the wood is wormy and looks too fragile to touch. Someone's home still has a hide and head of a snarling furry animal nailed to the inside of its door, even after thirty or more years. In one other room of this particular house, a weatherbeaten picnic table with benches attached is shoved into a corner of the kitchen and pieces of old wood clutter the whole area. But in this home at least the floor is wooden. In another the floor is dirt, hard-packed earth on which only squirrels and chipmunks play beside the single hoof and shinbone of a long dead and devoured deer. Was this artifact once part of a medicine man's sacred objects? If not, why was it saved? If so, why wasn't it taken?

Windows in another house are covered over with corrugated tin squares, painted creamy yellow and green a long time ago, but now faded into a noncolor. Wooden slats that were a roof have collapsed here, as well as in other homes, into the interior of the two-, three-, or four-room shacks so that birds homestead the open tops of the houses. In a few places, wooden ladders are nailed to the interior walls, creating a series of steps from the living rooms up to windows high in the lofts. Nervously chirping and flying in and out of the roof openings, myriad multicolored birds make the only sound heard at Whitetail on a windless day. No longer does children's laughter fill the air; no longer do the elders tell stories; no longer do campfires burn into the night; no longer do Apaches rest under the shelters at Whitetail; no longer do the spirits hear the prayers of a people accustomed to praying frequently during each day of their lives. No, today Whitetail is almost forgotten—neglected, left out in the open to endure the weather, to decay, and only sometimes to host special events such as private puberty ceremonies or prayer days arranged by spiritual leaders. For it is no longer acceptable to most Chiricahua Apaches to live where their ancestors did. These modern Americans want to be part of contemporary society; they want to live where good television reception is assured, where school bus access is easy for their children, near stores, gas stations, movies, church, and jobs. No one can blame them. Yet, for some present-day Apaches, such as Elbys Hugar and Kathleen Kanseah, Whitetail is still revered, still held close to their hearts, still visited on a regular basis, just to reflect and remember, and to recall the way it was when all the Chiricahua lived together in a small settlement high in the forest on the Mescalero Apache Reservation.

Elbys Naiche Hugar

I'm from a family that will be long remembered in many ways, not just because of my great-grandfather Cochise.

In brilliant sunshine, the Mescalero Apache Cultural Center awaits visitors. On a typical day, tourists from Europe, Mexico, and several states drive into the parking lot around tribal administrative offices and stop at a modest building. Identified only by a small sign, the one-story cultural center invites access through a brown-hued glass door. Most Apaches pass the building as they come and go during the day, picking up their mail at the nearby post office and tending to business at tribal headquarters. A few stop at the cultural center to chat from time to time, but Apache children are more often attracted to the museum: the fountain inside always provides an ice-cold drink of water for the kids on their way home from school. Frequently, an entire class of young Apache students from the elementary school, under the watchful eye of a teacher, come to the center to wend their way through the rooms and exhibits, and to view a videotape about their heritage. For many, the blood in their veins flows in a direct line from Cochise, Geronimo, Mangas Coloradas, Victorio, Juh, and other valiant Apaches. Today's kids squirm on cushions in the video theater at the cultural center and share the presentation with adult tourists listening to the rounded, melodious tones of the narrator, Wendell Chino. Mr. Chino has been chairman of the Mescalero Apache Tribe for nearly thirty-five years and is one of the most respected, yet controversial, Native American leaders in the nation. His talents as a storyteller, especially on the videotape played at the cultural center, are equally impressive.

When a visitor first enters the main room, ten life-sized mannequins wearing different traditional Apache costumes made by the elders are the welcoming party. So eye-catching is this display that Elbys Hugar, curator of this museum, is for the moment unnoticed. Sitting to the right of the exhibit at a worktable, or standing serenely behind a glass counter, the great-granddaughter of Cochise silently waits her turn for attention. This woman has been working at one job or another for the last forty years or

Elbys Naiche Hugar.
(Photo by H. Henrietta Stockel)

more. Once she was a bartender at the Tribal Lounge on the reservation, then she worked with the Traditional Apache Counselors and informed youngsters about the culture and traditions of her people. She taught the children the Apache names of different animals and how to write the Apache language. Also, she attended the Alamogordo (N.M.) Secretarial School and received a certificate as an executive secretary. Before she was transferred to the cultural center, she held a job at the rehabilitation center. "I worked here and there on the reservation. Different areas. That's the reason I'm familiar with a lot of things here on the reservation," she says modestly.

Elbys Hugar has a compelling family heritage of pride, courage, leadership, and physical prowess. Her great-grandfather, Cochise, described in an 1870 newspaper article as being

> five feet nine and one-half inches high; forty-six or forty-seven years old; weight 164 pounds; broad shoulders, stout frame; eyes medium size and very black; hair straight and black around arms; scarred all

over the body with buck-shot; very high forehead; large nose, and for an Indian straight,[12]

married the daughter of Mangas Coloradas, another notable chief, and at least two of their sons became prominent leaders. The ill-fated Taza, hand-picked by Cochise as his heir, died an untimely death from pneumonia in Washington, D.C., as he sought peace with the government after Cochise's death in 1874. "When Cochise got killed," says Mrs. Hugar, "Taza took over the Ch'ok'anande band and went to Washington in a delegation seeking peace. He caught pneumonia and died there. He is buried at the Congressional Cemetery in Washington. After that, my grandfather Naiche became chief." [13]

Most documents list Cochise's cause of death as cancer, which, according to Elbys Hugar, is incorrect. The famous chief's great-granddaughter insists the cavalry killed her ancestor, and she says it with such conviction that it is easy to believe her. "Cochise did not die of cancer," she said. "If he had cancer he would have taken care of it in an Indian way with Indian medicine. He got shot and killed. That's what my late father, Christian Naiche, Jr., said. And he would know. He was the grandson of Cochise and he himself told me how Cochise died. As soon as his people knew he was dead, they covered him up with rocks so that the white man wouldn't find his remains. His own people were the only ones who knew where he was buried."

Next in line behind Taza was Naiche, the tall, thin, quiet son of Cochise, who, with Geronimo and Lozen at his side, kept his people free from imprisonment for as long as was humanly possible. A measure of Naiche's greatness was his ability, in captivity, to remain a chief and, through his decisions on behalf of his people, to keep the harsh effects of imprisonment at a minimum.

While on the military reservation at Fort Sill, Naiche wholeheartedly embraced Christianity and served as an elder in the Reformed church. When the Chiricahua settled at Whitetail, Naiche, by then baptized and formally known as Christian Naiche, continued to lead his people, both religiously and secularly. One of Naiche's children with his wife, Ha-o-zinne, was also named Christian. He was Elbys Hugar's father.

Huera, wife of Mangus.
(Courtesy of Arizona Historical Society/Tucson, negative no. 25638)

Naiche and his wife Eh-clah-eh, parents of Dorothy Naiche.
(Courtesy of Museum of New Mexico, negative no. 15903)

"My grandfather Naiche had become a very religious man before he died," said Mrs. Hugar. "Also my father, Christian Naiche, Jr., went to the Reformed church at Whitetail a lot and I used to go with him. He talked about Jesus to us at home and who Jesus is and who his father, God, is. That's where I got to know the Bible. We learned a lot about believing in the Lord. My grandfather Naiche wrote an Apache hymn that the people still sing here at the Reformed church. Sometimes, when there's a gathering at the church, I go there and help sing in the Apache choir."

Like most Apaches, Mrs. Hugar prays frequently, wherever she may be. "I pray in my own language and ask for help and thank the Lord for helping me. We can pray in Apache at the church, if that's what we want, or we can pray in English. Whichever way we want to pray, we pray. The PERSON UP ABOVE understands. We pray to one person. That's the way we all believe. I pray for my relatives, my family, and the whole reservation here. When an Indian prays, they pray for everything and everyone. They not only pray for themselves, they pray for the poor, the sick, and for what we have here, what has been put here for us to enjoy—the pine trees, the fish in the creeks, good, fresh water, and the rainbow trout. We have a fish hatchery here on the reservation that stocks all the creeks and lakes."

Each time Elbys Hugar emerges from the cool shadow inside the cultural center to greet a visitor, her father's face, immortalized in a heavy, wooden-framed, enlarged, candid color photograph perched atop a small table behind the glass counter, seems to follow her. Christian Naiche, Jr., a shock of white hair framing his brown, wrinkled face, looks like the kindly grandfather everyone should have. Long ago he married a Mescalero Apache woman, Alta Treas, and fifty-nine years ago a baby girl arrived, one of seven children in the Christian Naiche, Jr., family: Sterling, Niles, Fidelia, Karis, Althea, Preston, and Elbys. "Preston was the youngest," said Elbys Hugar. "He fought in the Korean War as a sergeant. He lived here on the reservation all his life, and when he died there was a story written about his being in the straight bloodline of Cochise. He was a young man when he died, forty-seven years old, and he left his wife and seven children. There's nothing we can do about the bars that are open for Indians. That's how we lose some of our people when they are still young. From alcoholism. I lost a sister by that also."

Now Elbys Naiche Hugar is a small woman with curly black hair and large glasses. Polite, generous, and extremely diplomatic, with her family heritage and her easy way with strangers, Elbys Hugar is the perfect person to represent the Apache Tribe to tourists from throughout the world. Her legacy is leadership and she ably continues the tradition.

If Cochise walked in the door today, "I'd probably go to him and just put my arms around him and tell him who I am," she says, looking toward the cultural center's glass doors. And he probably would recognize her. Mrs. Hugar's eyes resemble Cochise's (and her grandfather Naiche's), as represented in a recently sculpted bronze bust. Other than the family's oral history, Elbys Hugar has no confidences about her ancestors that she discusses. Instead, she gladly recalls certain events from her younger years.

"They used to drive us children down from Whitetail and take us to the movies in Ruidoso to see Roy Rogers and Gene Autry fight the Indians," she chuckled. "I always wanted to meet those two fellows. Once, Gene Autry came to Ruidoso and sang at the library. I saw him. I always wanted to meet John Wayne, too, and that fellow who played Cochise, Jeff Chandler." [That was in *Broken Arrow*, a movie made many years ago. Elbys Hugar has seen it, naturally.] "The movie was made in more of a white way than an Indian way," she said. "The dancers were Navajos or the San Carlos Apaches, but they were not Chiricahuas who were singing and dancing in that movie. One of these days, if anyone makes a movie about Cochise again, I'd like to tell them a few things before they do. I know the real Cochise was a tall man," she said, "not thin or heavy set. One time a man asked how I felt about being related to a great man full of ambition for his people back in his time. I'm glad to say that I'm related to that man, and I'm proud to be part of him. My father talked about him many times, what kind of man he was, and said he always wanted to do things to help the people, not hurt them in any way, and that's the reason he wanted peace. With the way he was treated, it didn't work out, but Cochise knew he was right. It just seemed like they were always running. He wanted to make peace to save his people so that they could settle down and make a living, but there was always fighting."

History often tells another story. A document written by James H. Tevis, trading agent and manager of the Butterfield depot at Apache Pass on the

Bust of Cochise by sculptor Betty Butts, located at the National Hall of Fame for Famous Indians, Anadarko, Oklahoma.
(Photo by H. Henrietta Stockel)

Great Overland Mail Route, is one of a number of documented eyewitness accounts of Cochise and his band. Tevis wrote, "For eight months I have watched him and have come to the conclusion that he is the biggest liar in the Territory and would kill an American for any trifle, provided he thought it wouldn't be found out."[14]

Tevis's account is different from that reported by respected Apache agent Michael Steck, who, referring to Apache depredations, wrote in 1859, "there is no part of the whole extent where they have been less frequent within the last two years than in Arizona; yet from that quarter we hear the most complaint."[15]

One contemporary author described a series of raiding episodes carried out by Cochise's band in the years 1858–1861 and concluded that

> Cochise was not necessarily a scoundrel, but he has been misrep-resented. He has not been judged in terms of his own culture, but rather by Anglo-American standards. Herein lies the fault. . . . In the eyes of his followers, Cochise was both a general and a statesman, a superior individual who could outwit his enemies and continuously provide for the group.[16]

Regardless of whose account one chooses to believe, Mrs. Hugar speaks lovingly and convincingly of her ancestor, and as she continues talking about Apache people and Apache life, one falls under her spell and is led gently into another world. "I started working here in 1986," she said. "I enjoy talking with people who come from far away and telling about the history and the Apache people. I want others to get to know us because it seems that people who come to visit don't know much about the Apaches. Some of them ask me things that are very funny. Some of the visitors think that they are going to see Indians around here dressed in the Indian way, in a breechclout with arrows and paint and feathers. I tell them that it's not like that anymore, that we dress just like everybody else. The only time we wear our Indian clothing is when we have a feast going on, or danc-ing. People are surprised also because some of the Apache people are well educated and even the elderly speak the English language. But, anyway, I feel comfortable talking with them. They make me happy and I learn a lot about them, too. It's important that everyone knows the truth about everything here.

"I was born here at Mescalero," Mrs. Hugar said, "but later we lived with all the Chiricahua Indians at Whitetail. That's where I grew up. We worked in the fields after school. We worked in the gardens, learned how to put the seeds in the ground, how they grow, how to water them. It was very interesting to us children because we didn't know that you can put seeds in the ground and when they grow, have something to eat. My parents taught us how to plant the seeds. Back in those days, they used to get seeds from the agricultural department here on the reservation. The government gave out all kinds, even flower seeds. Free. Later we had to buy them, but when they were teaching us Apaches to plant gardens, that's when they gave us the seeds."

In her ties to the earth, Elbys Hugar follows a longtime tradition of connections between Apache women and agriculture. In olden times, girls accompanied their mothers and grandmothers as they all looked for "well over a hundred wild foods."[17] Youngsters were taught which were edible, which were utilized for healing, which had to be specially prepared, and which could be eaten raw.

> Under the scrutiny of their grandmothers, girls learned the intrica-
> cies of baking acorn bread in the ashes of a campfire. Both girls and
> boys were expected to learn how to cook meat in an edible fashion.
> Girls, however, were expected to learn all the varied intricacies of
> Chiricahua cuisine.[18]

Grenville Goodwin, a highly regarded chronicler of the Apache way, recorded his observations regarding Western Apache agriculture, but he couldn't capture the delight in a human voice that speaks with love of events long past.[19] As a youngster, Mrs. Hugar had a special connection with seeds, one that was important to her. "I remember one time when I ordered some garden seeds and flower seeds from a company. I used to sell them here on the reservation. When I collected the money after selling the seeds, I sent it back to the company. Then I got a prize. Jewelry or something. Anyway, I received a nice prize. I even used to sell Cloverine.

It was some kind of salve that had a good fragrance. It made your hands real soft and it smelled pretty." She smiled broadly.

Elbys Hugar is also a storyteller, one who is quite familiar with the history of her people. As she takes visitors to the cultural center through the various rooms, she points to photographs and artifacts and efficiently describes each one. "I remember many of these Apaches as elderly people on the reservation," she said. "There was nothing but elderlies here many, many years ago. Today you don't see hardly any, but back in those days you saw real old ladies carrying water or carrying wood or tanning hides, making moccasins, making baskets. I've seen a lot of them—real old people who did hard work and lived long, too. They all died of old age. That's the only way people died years ago, just of old age. But today there's a lot of sickness going around. Pneumonia, cancer, all kinds of disease among our people, and a lot of them die from it. That's why we don't have that many elderly people anymore. A lot of them die young because they get diseases."

Of compelling interest in the cultural center is an atrium with many various-sized black-and-white photographs of Apache people, especially Geronimo, and other shots of Daklugie, Chee, Enjady, Dahteste, Siki, Dorothy Naiche, and a group of Apache children at the Carlisle (Pa.) school. Mrs. Hugar's grandparents, Naiche and Ha-o-zinne, with their young daughter Jane and son Christian Naiche, Jr., snuggled up in a cradleboard, stare out of a photo at their granddaughter and the visitors. Mrs. Hugar is rather unique: not too many people are curators of museums in which their ancestors are featured.

Taking a tourist to a far corner of this room, Mrs. Hugar points to a larger-than-life ancient photo of an Apache family sitting in the dirt in front of a wickiup, a three-sided shelter used by the Apaches when they were nomads. "I remember something like that," she said. "Back in my young days we lived in tents, brush arbors, and tepees. We had a hard life. We had to carry our water from the creek and carry the wood from up in the mountains on our backs. We used it to cook and keep warm. We had to heat the water up outside by a fire to do our laundry and to take baths. But even though it was very hard to get by, we were all happy. We had a happy family."

From today's perspective, one wonders how in the world a people could be so poor and yet happy. "Because you feel more love," explained Elbys Hugar. "We all can feel it within each other—the warmth of what love really is when you are poor. Hardship keeps the family close together because all of us are in need and the only thing we have for each other is love. You can show your love more when you are poor, when you're really in need. You're always willing to help others. When our relatives came on a weekend to visit us, we brought the food out, what we had, and we ate with them. After we ate we talked, and the children played together. Those were the best days of my life."

Indian baseball was one of Elbys Hugar's favorite games at Whitetail. Unlike regular baseball, the Indian version features a ball made out of rags that is hit by the palm of the hand. "You throw it at the people, boys and girls or men and women. They run, all of them, to first base. There's a circle around the base and they all have to be inside that circle without getting hit. If one should get hit, that means they're out and they have to go back to home base and bat all over again until there are three outs and then they change sides. There's usually a dozen [players] on one team. It's a lot of fun. Sometimes, when they're running toward a base, you throw the ball and they dodge it. Then you have to run over there and pick up the ball. The ball is not that hard. That's why it didn't hurt when you got hit with that ball.

"We didn't have championships because we didn't really think about being champions and all that. We just played ball to have fun. That's the way Indian games are. All the Indian games are fun. That's what we want out of it, not the championship, not the competition.

"We used to play in the meadow at Whitetail and then they took us down to snake tank. It's about maybe ten miles from the school, down the road. There's a well there. That's where we went to play Indian baseball all the time because we liked it in an open area."

Mrs. Hugar smiles fondly at a memory coming back to her. "We made our own toys, too. I made a lot of rag dolls, even some out of plants. We used to make little tractors out of the spool of the thread. And we made slingshots. You know, with rubber."

While they were prisoners in Oklahoma, many of the Chiricahua learned how to run cows and grow crops. At Whitetail they continued these pursuits, but there wasn't very much money in beef at that time, so a few of the Chiricahua women worked to supplement their meager income. Mrs. Hugar remembers, "They called it 'gopher work.' The bus came to Whitetail and picked the women up. They had their lunch with them and the bus hauled them out in the boonies somewhere. They put carrots or something in the holes to kill the gophers. There were a lot of gophers at Whitetail. We were young and swimming in this dirty water one time. The women saw us and stopped. We jumped out of the water, grabbed our clothes, and started running. A little later, after they left, we went back in and were catching tadpoles. I told my mother about it that night before supper, while she was cooking. She said, 'Didn't you know that those tadpoles turn into frogs when they get big? If you carry them around and handle them with your hands, you are going to get warts all over your hands.' So she made us wash our hands with soap and water that night, hot water. It was fun, though. We all used to get together, play ball, go horseback riding, share garden and flower seeds, teach each other how to plant, and attend youth group meetings at the Apache Reformed Church at Whitetail. But we were so terribly poor."

Rich or poor, in those days every girl had a puberty ceremony, and Elbys Naiche was certainly no exception. "I had mine back in 1944," she said, "at the old ceremonial grounds. It's something good that a girl goes through. The parents and the godmother and the godfather talk with the young girl before the puberty ceremony. The girl will know what to do and she'll know about it before she can enter the ritual. If they don't know what they're doing, it's not going to work at all. They have to know what the ceremony is for and what the godmother is telling them. They should listen also to the godfather, and they will learn more about our traditional culture. It's for four days and nights. A girl has to fast, and sometimes you lose weight. That's what I experienced. It's still part of me and it's going to be that way for the rest of my life. I'll never forget the good it did for me and how it helped me over the hardships."

Elbys Hugar doesn't want to talk about the bad times in her life. Instead, she prefers to describe her mother, Alta Treas Naiche, and list the various traditional handicrafts she learned from her mother: beadwork, making cradleboards, moccasins, Indian dolls, leggings, and puberty clothing. "My mother was a very culturely lady who died in 1960, at sixty years of age. She spoke in Apache all the time and taught me a lot of Indian medicine, and Indian foods. We'd go out in the woods and stop by a plant. She'd tell me this is good for this, and this is good for that, and then she told me how to prepare the medicine. We'd go along a ways and see some more, and we'd stop there and she'd tell me some more about it. She knew a lot of plants to use for medicines for different kinds of diseases, and she talked a lot about how some of her people were saved from sicknesses by using Indian medicines for rheumatism, as an example. Nowadays the Indian ways of healing have become important to modern medicine because many people go through a lot. Stress, emotional things. And some people think they're sick when they're not. However, if someone really gets sick and they think they are not sick, they'll recover right away," she said. "This has worked for me many times. Another thing, you should never think about the past. Think about the future, how you're going to live happy, and think about the good things—your friends, your relatives. Think about the good side of them, don't think about the bad side. Maybe they've been in trouble or something happened to them a long time ago. Even if you know about these things, think about the good side of the people. Then, they'll gradually get better and turn themselves into a great person.

"That's why we believe in thinking about the good side of everybody, not what they did in the past. Maybe they used to drink heavily and today they have good homes. Be glad for them. They changed to the better way of life. Forget about their past. Everybody has done something wrong, you know. There's no one perfect. If you talk about people real good all the time and pray for them, they're going to be good people and they'll help you. That's the Apache way that my mother and father taught me.

"My mother also taught me how to sew. I can remember when my mother would make clothes for us out of feed sacks and flour sacks, the pretty flowered ones. She saved them and made dresses and blouses for us. That's what we used to wear to go to school. She sewed them by hand, and later the government was giving out Singer sewing machines. She had one and later on used to sew with it, but I took a sewing class. The school

Ha-o-zinne, grandmother of Elbys Naiche Hugar.
(Courtesy of Fort Sill Museum, Fort Sill, Oklahoma, photograph no. P3602)

used to take us to El Paso to that class, where I learned how to make quilts and dresses. We used to get materials and threads and things like that in El Paso. It was cheaper there. I was ashamed of my shoes, but I used to wear them all the way to El Paso." [Shoes?] "Yes, the government gave us a pair of high-topped black shoes with laces clear to the top. Some of us cut them down to the ankles, like slippers, and some just wore them like they were. When I was old enough to go to school in a pair of shoes like that, I cut mine down. I was ashamed of them. Not too long ago I sewed a puberty dress for my granddaughter, Janice Enjady, and she had her feast in it about two years ago. I'm planning on making another one for my other granddaughter, Kimberly, for her ritual ceremony."

If she were to make these beautiful buckskin dresses for all of her grandchildren, Elbys Hugar would probably have time for nothing else. She has five sons and two living daughters from her first marriage, and seven stepchildren from her second marriage.

"I got married for the first time in 1952," she said. "Since I was marrying a man from another culture, I thought it was best that I got married in a white way, by a justice of the peace. When I was a little girl I used to listen to the Grand Old Opry on the radio and, I don't know why, but I always prayed that I would meet someone from there [Nashville] so that I might some day see it in person. My first husband was from Cookville, Tennessee; I met him at Holloman Air Force Base in New Mexico. Both of us were young when we got married, and we had all the children. In those days, we didn't have Pampers. I used Birds' Eye diapers and I washed them by hand in a galvanized tub with a washboard. That's how I did my laundry many times.

"I started off living in an old house—a shack—on the reservation. I used a woodstove, carried my water, and just stayed home and took care of the house and the children. I don't like to talk about this, but I got a divorce back in 1966."

Charles Hugar, Elby's husband, is a retired army sergeant who was in the armed forces for over twenty-three years and served his country in Korea and Vietnam. A native of Altoona, Pennsylvania, he met his future wife while she was spending time with relatives in Apache, Oklahoma. In

1971 they were married in the Reformed church at Apache by the Reverend Andy Kamphins, and subsequently they returned to Mescalero to live their life. "We're happy together," Elbys Hugar said. "He taught me many things I didn't learn from my first husband. I really grew up when I married Charles Hugar. I got to know a lot of things from him. When I was growing up and in school I didn't talk the way I do now. I was very shy. I'm just a quiet person. My husband and I traveled every now and then, and that's where I got over my shyness. When I first married him he was a salesman, insurance and life salesman, and one night they invited him to go to a big restaurant to eat. All the families went and he sat with me right in the middle of those people. I said to him, 'Let's sit over here in the corner.' And he said, 'No, we're going to sit over here, right in the middle.' That's when I learned how to be among people. Now I can go anywhere before a crowd and talk with them and answer questions— whatever they ask me—and I love to talk with people today. I thought to myself later, 'Why was I afraid of these people?' I'm glad I got over that feeling. My husband taught me how to live among people in the way I am now. I'm always willing to talk with anyone.

"Charles is a bookworm; he reads all the time, and he's a very intelligent man. We've been back here on the reservation for about seventeen years now. We have our own home, a TV set (which I didn't have before), and I'm happy with him. All my children are married also now. They all have their own families and they all have jobs, and they are living good here on the reservation. I'm very proud of all my children; I love all of them. They're part of me, part of my blood, clear back from Cochise's blood.

"Two of my children have their own businesses. My oldest son, Jack Blaylock, is a contractor and builds homes. He reminds me of Cochise; he's tall and husky. My oldest daughter, Joyce Waters, has her own beauty shop. My daughter Debbie finished computer study in Albuquerque; one of my boys, James, is a conservation officer. I had a set of twins, but I lost the girl from a heart murmur when she was two months old. The other twin, Dennis, is a carpenter working at the reservation's sawmill right now; Ronald is working there, too. Troy, the youngest boy, is also a carpenter and he works sometimes with Jack, building and repairing homes.

They all grew up with hardship; that's where they learned to work and to earn for their family. That's why they're all working today, why they have their homes, and why they take care of their families."

Elbys Hugar credits her mother with teaching her how to rear her children. "My mother taught us respect," she said, adding, "how to respect the people. There's different ways in respect. One way is your son-in-law. When a woman respects her son-in-law, she cannot see him. She always covers her head with a blanket when he's around and she never talks to him. When we lived in Whitetail, we didn't have anything at all to travel in. Later, they gave out horses. Later, my father bought a Model-A Ford and we used to come down to the agency in that Model-A Ford, but we had to have a piece of cloth hanging in the middle of the car, between the front seat and the back seat, because of my grandmother. She had respect for my father, her son-in-law, and the cloth hanging in the middle meant she couldn't see him and couldn't talk to him. If she should be out somewhere and one of the grandchildren told her that their daddy was coming, she'd cover her head. It's a respect that they have in an Indian way for the mother-in-law not to see the son-in-law or talk to him. That's the way we traveled all the time when we'd take my grandmother.

"Back in those days women never drove a car. I never heard of a woman driver until maybe in the past thirty years. I drive now, too. It was very hard for me to learn how to drive because of those big semi trucks. I get scared. They made me nervous at first, but later I got used to them. Now, I drive around all the time. It doesn't bother me. But I don't like to drive where there's a lot of traffic. So my husband does the driving when we go to Albuquerque."

Mrs. Hugar continued talking about the Apache tradition of respect. "The other way is to have respect for one another and for the people. There is also another respect that we have—never say a bad word in front of your brother or your father, and also never change your clothes in front of your brother or your father. I still live that way. There's a lot of words I don't say in front of my husband, my sister. There's things I don't say at all because they might be out of the way. With respect, I don't say these things. Even to some of my friends, and some of the important people who live here on the reservation that we talk with today, I always respect them and don't say anything out of the way to them.

"Another thing, I always have to watch what I say all the time," she added. "You really have to watch it when you are a true Indian. There is something within yourself that you hold for your people in respect. You're always going to have it with you. It will be there all the time. And that's what I have within me.

"I treat my sons with respect. I never change clothes in front of them, I never say a bad word in front of them. I have a lot of respect for my sons because I love each one and I think they should know that by having this respect for them, they'll carry it on and they will also have respect in many ways."

Mrs. Hugar taught her children the same way her mother taught her. She has passed on the Apache traditions. "I taught my daughters most of the things I know," she said, "but there's still some I need to tell them about. It's a lifelong process because you bring this out a little at a time, not everything at one time. And there's a reason for that. There are some that come with the seasons. Like Indian foods. You have to gather these in the fall. Indian medicines have the blooms on them in May. That's when you teach the children what's good for this and what's good for that, and how to identify them. In winter, you teach them how to make jerky. It all depends on the time of year. These are the old ways. It takes time to learn everything. In a year's time you can't learn everything. It takes a long time, and learning goes like a clock. We Apaches always start at the east where the sun comes up. Never start backwards; always start clockwise. My mother and father taught me this.

"There's a lot of times that I want to bring something out in English to those people who do not understand the Apache language. But it's very hard to try to get to the point that you're trying to explain. If you say it in Indian to another person who understands the language—the Apache language, that is—it's easy because the person knows what you're talking about. If you try to bring it out in English, it's very hard."

Because of her deep beliefs and her regard for tradition, Mrs. Hugar has made an incomparable contribution to the Apache culture and people:

she is coauthor of the only Mescalero Apache dictionary. As in all things, she is modest about this striking accomplishment. "We want to keep our language alive," she says simply. "That's why we wrote the dictionary." Arranged by topic, the red-covered reference book is used "from kindergarten on up to the sixth grade to teach our language to our children." Plans are now under way to produce a second volume addressing verbs only. This book may be put on tape for cassette players.

"I always wanted to give something to my tribe, to the people. I wanted to let them know that I'm from a family that will be long remembered in many ways, not just because of my great-grandfather Cochise. I also want to give part of myself to the people who come by the cultural center. When they ask me things, I want to always give them the answers, the true answers. I talk many times to students, and when there are meetings at the community center, I'm there to give a little advice to the people. I tell them that we need to keep our culture, the traditions, and the language. The language is the main thing that we must keep, and so I helped compile the dictionary for the tribe.

"Nowadays most of the young children speak only the English language, and they don't know the Apache language that comes from the heart of all the people. I had a hard time learning English because I speak Apache fluently. I didn't know a word of English when I started school. One time my mother beaded a little cradle for me to take to the grocery store to sell. She said, 'Give this to the storekeeper and tell him to give you fifty cents for this cradle. If he tells you twenty-five cents, tell him you want fifty cents.' I didn't know what money was in those days, either. The storekeeper told me, 'I'll give you a dollar for this.' I told him, 'No, I want fifty cents.' So, he gave me fifty cents. That's how much I knew. Later, I learned how to read and write in English, and today I can laugh about that incident."

At Whitetail, Elbys Hugar and other Apache children attended the same schoolhouse that stands vacant today. "We learned the basics up there," she said. "Reading, writing, spelling, arithmetic, and geography. First grade on up to eighth grade, and then I had to go off to a boarding school because there was no higher school here at that time. I went to the Albuquerque Indian School with a lot of Pueblo Indians and a lot of Navajos. There was one Hopi Indian in my class, too. It was very hard. Nowadays,

I notice that some of the students who graduate still don't know how to read, pronounce a word, or spell. A lot of them don't know geography. They don't even know what continent they're living on, even after they graduate." According to Mrs. Hugar, it wasn't that way at Whitetail, where learning also consisted of religious education. "Every Thursday afternoon the minister and his wife came to have a little church service," she remembered. "They gave us a chapter in the Bible to read and others to look up. We had to memorize some of the verses. I'm glad that I learned these things so I can pass them on to my children and other people. This is very important to me. I have love for my people here on the reservation, especially the children, those here and those yet to come. I'm very grateful that I'm the great-granddaughter of Cochise, and I don't want my heritage and that of the Apache people to vanish.

"What needs to be done in young marriages is for the parents to speak the Apache language at home and teach their children the traditions and culture. If they don't, it's going to be gone later."

And what of the ceremonies and rituals? The customs? Does Elbys Hugar worry that they are endangered as well? "We should think more about our traditional culture," she replied. "Once you're an Indian, you're always an Indian. Maybe you can change your ways. Dress different. Dress like the modern ways and change your attitude to be more in the modern way. But you can also hang onto your culture if you really believe in the traditions. It's going to help you and you can pray in this way. In the Indian way. Pray that you want to keep this [the traditions] and it will be a part of you. This feeling [of being Indian] is the greatest thing that we need to hang onto. If you don't practice your traditions, you're going to lose them. If you don't live like the old ways every once in a while, you're going to lose your culture. The best way to keep it is the feelings you have within yourself that you're an Indian. Because once you're an Indian, you're always going to be an Indian. You have the blood of an Indian. We are all Apache people; we should keep this inside of us . . . learn the culture . . . the Apache way. It's just part of being an Indian that's within the person."

For instance, the custom concerning the belongings of people who have just died is one that continues to be observed today. Is it in danger of being lost through lack of use? No, not yet, according to Elbys Hugar, who says, "We believe that if we keep something that belonged to the person who died, it will bother us afterwards. We throw everything away that belonged to them. If a person should die in a home and they have a lot of furniture, dishes, and other things, the family throws them all away or gives them away. They throw clothing away or burn all of it. The close relatives won't take the things, but you offer it to them but they don't want it in the family." Why? "Because the spirit will be bothering them. The way we believe, the spirit keeps coming back and wants the things. That's why we don't keep any of the belongings."

And what of the traditional language? "Once we learn the language, it's there. We will never part from it. Like myself. I was brought up in a poor home but in a culturely way, and I learned some of the traditions. From my mother and from my father. He sang a lot of songs; he was a medicine man, he sang the Mountain Spirit dancer songs and the Apache war dance song. Some of the young men have learned how to sing it and are carrying it on today. We need to give the language, the traditions, the songs to the young people so they can keep them around all the time for the Apache people."

Other people care as much as Elbys Hugar does. "My age group," she said, "they think the way I do. We all grew up in the same way. No one was richer than the other, no one had more than the other, and we all helped one another. We all lived the same way—poor. My age group are the ones that know the culturely things and the traditions. I'm not the only one thinking that I want the children to carry on the traditions, the culture, and the language.

"Young people do not understand this today. They need to sit down with relatives, their parents, and learn these ways of our people. Later on there will be no one to talk like this to them. The young people need advice in an Indian way. We don't give advice like the white people do. When we bring up a subject in our own language, there's something there. If they can, the younger generation will take it within themselves, will feel it from the elderly, when they are talking about something together. It's not going to happen in English. That's why we want the young people to speak the Apache language."

It seems that Elbys Hugar is living in two worlds, the old and the new. Is it really possible for her to hold the culture in her heart, be completely modern, and yet be a traditional Apache? "Yes," she said. "That's the way I am. I know I'm an Indian. I have royal blood inside of me from Cochise, and it will remain with me forever. Even though I speak the English language and I live the ways of the white people, I'm still an Indian. I have that feeling and it's going to be there all the time.

"My children are half Indians, and proud of it. I explained all of this to them and they believe the same way I do. They live both ways also. Some of them tan deer hides. Some of them love Indian crafts. One of them, my oldest son, helps the medicine man with the *Gah'e*. He didn't know a word of Apache, but now he sings in Apache for the *Gah'e*. He has learned a lot of the traditions from the medicine man, and he is very glad and proud of himself for this."

And, speaking of ceremonies, Elbys Hugar is looking forward to next year's puberty ceremony when her granddaughter will be one of the maidens participating. "Hopefully, we'll have everything ready by then. I'm making her dress. Before I start it, I pray, and then I go through it. Before you know it, the dress is finished. Everything is done by hand. All the beadwork, everything," she says, as she happily plans to pass on the Apache traditions to subsequent generations of her family—just as they were passed to her from her mother, grandmother, and great-grandmother, Toos-day-zay, the wife of Cochise.

Not much is known about the daughter of Chief Mangas Coloradas, the woman who became Cochise's wife and then the mother of Naiche, but this much is certain: as the daughter of one chief and the wife of another, she had leadership qualities herself and undoubtedly knew how to exercise them appropriately. After all the years of imprisonment, her son Naiche brought her with him to Whitetail, where she lived quietly among family members and friends.

Many of the descendants of those Chiricahuas were in Anadarko, Oklahoma, during the first week of August 1989 when a bronze bust of Cochise was presented by its sculptor, Betty Butts, to the National Hall of Fame for Famous Indians.

Naturally, Elbys Hugar was the featured speaker, but just days before she was scheduled to formally thank Ms. Butts, Elbys's voice deserted her. "That's because she has to give a speech and she hates to do that," said husband Charles Hugar with a grin on his face. "Not so," she protested. Elbys and Charles Hugar drove the twelve-hour trip from Mescalero to Anadarko in their van and stayed with relatives in the area. She decided to wear a red "camp dress," her ceremonial dress, to the presentation of the bust. Around her neck Mrs. Hugar wrapped a bone, mescal bean, and shell necklace she made herself; it fell to her waist. And on her feet she wore beaded moccasins with the characteristic toe guard distinctive of the Chiricahua people.

After the event's opening formalities, outdoors under a brush arbor, the chief of the Mescalero Tribe, Wendell Chino, described Cochise, the man and the leader. It was a rare time, one when a current chief, himself a descendant of Geronimo, honored another, long deceased. Mr. Chino's words were carefully chosen, befitting a man of his status. "With 32 years as head of his tribe, Wendell Chino has been in office longer than any other Indian chief," said a recent article.

> His record is nothing short of remarkable. He has parlayed the pragmatic survival skills and resourcefulness of his people into a modern style so shrewd and intimidating it would be the envy of any corporate raider. . . . Here is a man who has taken his people's concerns to the Supreme Court and won, cowed the federal Bureau of Indian Affairs (BIA) and challenged state and federal agencies again and again, leaving them licking their wounds. He seems to have the warrior's atavistic ability to press on and on.[20]

In melodious tones, Chairman Chino praised the Apache Cochise as a man of peace, not war. His voice grew louder as he described several events in Cochise's life and further depicted the adversities and hardships suffered by all Apache people under the rule of the dominant culture's government. The audience, sitting on hard wooden benches in 108-degree heat with 94 percent humidity, didn't blink. The chairman rocked back and forth on his heels, shoved the microphone aside, and grew even more eloquent, jabbing his finger into the air as he made his statements. No one, not even those belonging to the "dominant culture" in the gathering, would have challenged him. When his oration was over, Mr. Chino dropped his voice and introduced the descendants of Cochise. One by one they rose from the bench, proud and tall, women and men, children too, and gave everyone a smile. As the chairman called their names, it seemed his voice rolled across the green hills of Oklahoma. Mr. Chino then asked Elbys Hugar to approach the microphone. She and her daughter, Debbie Enjady, presented a turquoise necklace to the sculptor. Debbie spoke for her mother, but Mrs. Hugar managed to whisper a few hoarse words. Then the entire presentation continued with the Hall of Fame officials making speeches and introducing their board members.

The sun ducked in and out of the clouds, but finally gleamed brightly on the bronze bust of Cochise, now blessed with yellow pollen by a Mescalero Apache medicine man also related to the great warrior. In the words of the sculptor, Betty Butts, Cochise "seemed to be taking it all in." She pointed out that no matter where one stood, Cochise's eyes followed.

After the ceremony, Mrs. Hugar posed for photos and then modestly slipped away amid her family. Enough fanfare. The Apache ambassador, a direct descendant of the mighty and valiant Cochise, was eager to return to New Mexico and to her work in the Mescalero Apache Cultural Center.

Kathleen Smith Kanseah

*One thing I've learned about being an Apache woman is
that you sit back and listen, you keep your eyes open and your
mouth shut . . .*

Not too far off the westbound lane of the federal highway
that bisects the Mescalero Apache Reservation, Kathleen Kanseah's red
house is well secluded in a thick forest setting. A white stone chimney
reaches above the trees, just as she described when giving directions, but
it takes a driver a few long seconds to recognize the spot. Side by side
with a barn, the house has a welcome feel to it, especially when Kathleen
waits inside the storm door, a smile filling her dimpled face. (According
to one member of the Fort Sill Apache Tribe, Geronimo had dimples,[21]
but Kathleen Kanseah has never claimed the warrior as her ancestor.) If
it is late in the afternoon or a weekend, two granddaughters will always
be nearby. One usually hears them first. Then they appear. Six-year-old
Marlys and eight-year-old Theresa are happy youngsters, full of life and
fun. There is nothing shy about them, nothing fearful, and nothing that
would cause them to be awkward or self-conscious. They are pixies in the
woods, allowed to be totally themselves, free spirits, loved unconditionally
by their grandmother.

And Kathleen does love them dearly. It shows in the way she respects
them by talking softly with them, not at them. She doesn't raise her voice.
She reasons. She gives them instructions, yes, and from time to time has
to put a hard edge to her voice to convey seriousness, but she does all this
with an implicit assurance of love. For instance: white sneakers soaked in
mud. It had rained heavily in the canyon and Marlys was outside playing
with her sister. She appeared at the door and looked down at her feet.
The shoes, previously little-girl grimy white, were minus their laces, mud
brown, and sopping wet. Marlys marched in the house and called attention
to her feet by standing absolutely still just inside the door and staring at
the floor. Kindly, patiently, Kathleen asked what happened to the sneakers,
and Marlys said, "Mud." That was all. There was no yelling, no repri-

mand, no disciplinary action, no "I told you not to play in the mud" from Grandma. "Take them off and leave them outside," said Kathleen. "We'll wash them later." Marlys skipped back out the door and did as she was told, coming into the house immediately thereafter and putting on another pair of shoes. "Oh, those girls," said Kathleen, with gentle patience. "They're a handful." [22]

Kathleen has custody of the girls and is rearing them in the same way she reared her two sons—intelligently and with feeling. Her husband was Lee Kanseah, the son of Jasper Kanseah, one of the young boys in Geronimo's band. Jasper was about thirteen years old when Geronimo surrendered, and he is shown in the widely publicized photo of the Chiricahua people sitting on a small hill outside the train taking them to prison. On her side of the family, her father was Hopkins Smith, Sr., and her mother was Martina Little. "My mother was Spanish," said Kathleen, "but from what I hear, one of her ancestors was captured in Tularosa [New Mexico] by the Apaches. My grandfather used to do a lot of work with the tribe. He had land in La Luz and in Tularosa and down in Three Rivers. He and my grandmother lived right inside the reservation. The adobe house they had is still up. When they were enrolling people into the tribe, they asked my grandparents if they would enroll their children. I think there were five or six of them in the family at that time. From what I understand, it was an act of Congress to get them enrolled into the tribe because they had Spanish blood.

"My mother's family was raised with the Apaches. My mother spoke Indian fluently, and so did the rest of the family except Uncle Paul and Uncle Mike, my mother's brothers, even though Uncle Mike went to school at Carlisle with the other Apache students." [23]

Kathleen's grandfather, Oswald Smith, was born in 1871 with the Apache name Chez-lo-teed-lay. On November 4, 1886, he entered the Carlisle school and remained there until March 26, 1894, when he was sent to Mount Vernon, Alabama, to join other imprisoned Apaches. Oswald Smith was moved to Fort Sill from Mount Vernon and began to work at the Dutch Reformed Mission. In 1913 he was released from prison and subsequently made his home at Mescalero, where he died after being struck by lightning. Kathleen's grandmother, Gertrude Smith, was born in 1884,

Kathleen Smith Kanseah.
(Photo by H. Henrietta Stockel)

the daughter of Go-lah-ah-tsa and her husband, Clee-neh. Gertrude Smith was a full sister of Richard Imach, the father of Mildred Cleghorn, who is currently the chairperson of the Fort Sill Apache Tribe. Kathleen Kanseah's grandmother thus is Mildred Cleghorn's aunt.

Family relationships are important to most Apaches, and many are acutely aware of the names of their ancestors, especially those whose relatives were prisoners of war. During a trip to Apache, Oklahoma, and the surrounding area, Kathleen Kanseah stood silently in the September morning sun for a long time in front of the Fort Sill Apache Cemetery grave of her great-grandmother, Go-lah-ah-tsa, and bowed her head. Occasionally, she would put one foot in front of the other as a start in walking away, but she remained in place, deep in thought, eyes lowered. When she was able, she turned toward the other graves and slowly made her way among the rows, reading epitaphs on the individual gravestones. It was obvious from her expression that she was dismayed and disgusted at the damage done to many of the granite markers by soldiers riding grass-cutting machines. Portions of letters in names or dates had been obliterated through this carelessness, but Kathleen kept her silence until she read a name on one stone and the engraving under it that said simply, "Apache Woman." She frowned and asked rhetorically, "Is that all they could say? Didn't this woman have any relatives? Any friends? Someone must have been part of her life."

Those words were representative of a century of a people's frustration, exasperation, indignation, anger, and rage at government officials and an official U.S. policy that endorsed and supported the incarceration of another independent nation—because their way of life interfered with the wishes of the "dominant culture." True, the circumstances during the days of the frontier West may have been quite complex, but the actions of the military speak for themselves across the decades. As only one example: Apache scouts, loyal and faithful to the U.S. Army, even at the risk of being considered traitors by their people, were rewarded by being imprisoned with all other Apaches and treated the same as those labeled hostiles.

Today, at Fort Sill, the difference between the post cemetery where soldiers and their families rest, and the Apache cemetery is quite revealing. The former is neatly groomed and centrally located on the grounds. It is

Apache women of the future: Marlys (left) and Theresa Smith.
(Photo by H. Henrietta Stockel)

easy for relatives to find and visit. In contrast, the Apache cemetery looks ragged—not exactly unkempt but certainly not tidy—and badly needs attention. Graves of recently deceased Apaches still wait to be marked, even though they are three or four years old. The site is distant from the center of activities, but not too far from the firing range. The sound of cannon fire exploding nearby constantly disturbs the solemnity.

It is too easy to reach obvious conclusions, even for Apache woman Kathleen Kanseah, who, with hurt in her eyes and heart, said, "The trees look healthy and it is peaceful here. I wish they would do something about that big anthill, though."[24]

At the Lawton Public Library, less than twenty-five miles from Fort Sill, Kathleen studied a document describing the medical histories of some Apache prisoners of war.[25] Page after page of the army records list births and deaths, always with the preface "APW" (Apache Prisoner of War).

For the Smith family, as an example, there is an entry concerning a female child named Lizzie, born on October 19, 1903, the third child of

Kathleen's grandparents Gertrude and Oswald. Sadly, another listing reveals that she died one month and seventeen days later, on November 26, 1903, of unknown causes. On June 11, 1905, the fourth child of Gertrude and Oswald was born and named Louise. John Smith, aged sixteen years six months, died October 20, 1905, from acute tuberculosis.[26]

Other families are also well represented in the lists of vital statistics, but the deaths of so many children haunt a reader, as do the gravestones at the Apache cemetery. One family lost five children in one year, and it is difficult to imagine how the parents had the will to continue to survive. That more wives were taken and more children born is testimony to the enduring spirit of the Apache nation and to the compelling desire of a people to keep their name from vanishing.

An entry concerning the illness rampant on the post was made on March 31, 1904:

> The sickness among the Apache Prisoners of War is on the increase, as may appear from the number remaining in hospital. The increase in hospital is due to a desire on the part of the sick to take treatment in the hospital, rather than at their villages, as had been their habit. W. M. Roberts, AA Surg.[27]

The medical records also contain census information. In October 1904 there were 232 Apache prisoners of war—55 men, 48 women, and 99 children.[28] One of the last entries is dated April 2, 1913: "187 Apache Prisoners of War released and turned over to the Indian Department and departed for Mescalero Agency, New Mexico; accompanied by 1st Lt. Thomas L. Ferenbaugh, M.C."[29]

From time to time Kathleen had to stop reading. She looked up at nothing in particular and munched on a peppermint. Then she continued reading until finally she had to stop. "It seems such a shame," she said. "So much sickness, so much death."[30]

Kathleen herself was born at Mescalero a little more than sixty years ago (she won't give her exact age) and attended boarding school on the reservation for a short period of time. "I guess my mother didn't like what was going on so she took me out and put me in the public school. It was just a one-room classroom down across from the Reformed church. I went to school there from the first until the sixth grade.[31]

"We used to live where the Reformed church camp is now in a four-room frame house. From there we moved up to where the minister has his house now. That's where they used to have a three-bedroom government home that we moved into. My mother worked for the government and my father was a policeman at one time for the tribe. They didn't allow children to go to the public school with the Anglos, but I was allowed to go when my mother started working at the hospital as a government employee. My brother and I went to school there.

"Then one year my brother and I went to the Santa Fe Indian School, and when we came back we both finished in Tularosa at the high school. We went on the school bus that ran from Mescalero down to the old Bent Post Office, and picked up kids in Tularosa also. There was no "athletic bus" at that time, and my brother used to play football in Tularosa. He'd have to hitchhike home every day after school [a distance of more than twenty miles]. He struggled through that until he went into the navy. When I graduated I went into nurses' training in Oklahoma and became an LPN. I went to Minnesota and worked as an LPN and took a semester of evening courses to see if I could get my RN, but the business of Indian education was a problem, so I didn't continue. I transferred back to New Mexico and worked at Crownpoint, among the Navajo, as an LPN [Licensed Practical Nurse].

"I was there for six months when my mother became deathly ill, so I came home to Mescalero and worked at the hospital for three years. Then I asked for a transfer to Santa Fe and worked almost twelve years at the Indian hospital there. Four of us traveled back and forth to Albuquerque to take courses at the university. We'd get home from school about 10:00 at night. I'd get myself dressed and go to work at midnight, get back to the house about 9:30 in the morning, sleep until noon, and then dig into the books. I had four kids going to school at the same time and a husband working in Santa Fe. He worked only part time because he had injured his back, but he did a lot of work for me at home. Then we brought my mother up to Santa Fe from Mescalero because she was going blind and she was a severe diabetic. She was a lot of help with the kids.

"Then I had a chance to go to a physician's assistant course in Phoenix, Arizona. I went down there for an interview and I was accepted. When I was ready to go, my mother got terribly sick and then my husband got deathly ill. I just called Phoenix and canceled the whole thing. They were trying to tell me something, I believe. So I stayed home with my mother for a year and then she passed away."

While speaking about her youth, Kathleen Kanseah recalled that she did not have a puberty ceremony when she was a young woman, and today she says, "That was terrible. I regret it. I really regret it. But old man Eugene Chihuahua gave me his blessings for two days down at the house there by the community center. I can still hear him. He said, "You're my grand-daughter now. For two nights I'll sing for you and bless you and get you going because you're going to be a very strong woman." I was twelve or thirteen years old when he said that, and he had me sitting on the ground on a tarp. My father put the sacred pollen on him, I put the pollen on him, and then he put pollen on me. I can still hear his songs. He was a very powerful man, and he told me I would be a strong woman. And I find that I can be strong in a lot of things."

With her family needing her as much as they did, Kathleen indeed ful-filled the revered medicine man's prediction. Despite the demands on her, however, she kept a delightful sense of humor and today enjoys telling stories about the way things were when she was a child. A favorite is about an experience she had at Whitetail. "I must have been three or four years old," she said, "and I remember everybody running in all directions, even my grandmother Gertrude Smith Shanta, who was a heavyset woman. My uncle Willis picked me up and put me over his shoulders and told me to hang on to his head because he didn't want to leave me there by myself. I was hanging on for dear life, and he ran behind the outhouse along the edge of the mountain, asking 'Do you see it? Do you see it?' Well, I finally saw this white thing running with its tail sticking up, and I didn't know what kind of animal it was that everybody was chasing. Well, it was a white skunk! I never saw one again."

And she has a similar amusing remembrance from her days working as an LPN in Minnesota among the Chippewa Indians twenty miles north-west of Duluth. "My friend and I were at her place," Kathleen recalled, "and we had to go down and pick her father up at the paper mill. Her brother didn't tell her that he had run over a skunk with the car, so while we were driving down the road, it smelled bad. It was twenty degrees below zero and we had to roll the windows down. Her father was waiting for us and he smelled it, too. He stood on the side of the car and said, 'I'm not riding home with you girls. I'll catch a ride.' He wouldn't get into the car, and we had to go back up the highway alone, still with the windows rolled down in the freezing night. Oh, that was a horrible smell."

Telling these stories produced others about some experiences she had during her nursing career. One memory in particular, from her days at the Santa Fe Indian Hospital, amused her. "One of the nurses always laughed at me because I could tell which tribe a patient was from by the food that was eaten. The Pueblo people ate the fruit and bread and some of the vegetables, but very little bread. The Apaches ate meat, potatoes, and bread. And coffee. Apaches love their coffee. The Plains Indians ate meat and bread." Kathleen Kanseah's chuckle brightened the room. She is an Apache woman who fits comfortably in the traditional and modern worlds, sometimes simultaneously.

"I lived on the outside world from the time I was in grade school and I went into public school. I wasn't in contact with a lot of Apaches, but I played on weekends with children my age. I lived with the white people, worked with them, went to school with them, and then when feast time came, or there was something going on, we all came home. Or like we used to say, 'We come back to the blanket.' There's always something that draws you back to this spot right here." She leaned across the kitchen table and pointed her finger toward the window.

Listening to her talk with great affection about the Mescalero Reservation, one gets the impression that Kathleen Kanseah has a tremendous store of knowledge about the old ways and is very protective of tradition. "One thing I've learned about being an Apache woman," she says, "is that you sit back and listen, you keep your eyes open and your mouth shut, especially when you're way out somewhere in strange territory, or even among your own people. You have to be careful when you speak, you have to watch what you say to different ones. If you're an Apache, something inside will tell you. Silent communication. You know who you can talk to, who you can tease. The majority of them you can tease and joke with, but there's some you cannot. Some of them are very sensitive about things.

"My grandmother used to tell me, 'Don't speak until you're spoken to.' You stand back. If you want to be a true Indian and a proud Indian, you stand back. You stand there and you listen and you keep your eyes open but keep your mouth shut. You do not speak until someone asks you something. If you can answer, you answer. If not, you don't say anything. I've told my girls that by observing, you learn a lot. Always keep your eyes open. Look for everything. Look around. Look at what's around you. Look at the good things around, good things like the flowers and the trees, the animals and pretty people. Things like that.

"I tell my girls to keep quiet and keep their eyes open. At the puberty ceremony they observed everything that was going on. They learned from that. I told them that when they go to the ceremony to eat, they should eat only what they can. I told them not to fill up the plate, to just take what they can eat. I said that if they got a piece of fry bread, they had to eat all that bread. I told them they couldn't break it or leave it. One day Theresa asked, 'Why not break the fry bread, Grandma, and eat half?' I told her that the bread is a circle, the circle is life, bread is life. If it's a big piece, they can nibble on it, but they can't throw it away.

"I told them too that when they were dancing with the *Gah'e*, the fire dancers, that they had to watch the fire. The fire tells you a lot of things. If you're praying hard enough, you can see a lot of things in the fires. I told the girls that they shouldn't be going out there just to be dancing around for pleasure. Sure, there's a little pleasure in a lot of things, but the main thing when you're dancing with the fire dancers is to have respect for them. They do a lot of praying and a lot of things that youngsters don't realize, but later on in life they'll find out.

"My grandmother used to tell me to watch the dancers, and when they sweat and all that paint comes off, she said that showed they have really put their whole heart in what they're doing. 'They're praying,' she said. That's why they were sweating."

Kathleen Kanseah dances with the *Gah'e* every chance she gets. "As long as the Good Lord lets me, I'll keep dancing," she says with a wide grin. "I'll keep going, just like the maidens in the tepee during the puberty ceremony. That's another thing. You can always tell what kind of a woman the maiden will be by the way she dances. For some, it's so easy. No problem. Other girls slouch around. You can predict.

"What I see with the young people today is that the parents don't bother to teach the kids the old ways. But then there are so many people who used to be alcoholics and they never taught their kids. That's where they lost it. That's the sad part—the middle group between the youngsters and the old people. I feel sorry for them; even though they have been taught some of the culture they have not carried it to their kids. The kids are living now in the white man's way because of their parents' alcoholism."

Not Theresa and Marlys, though, and not as long as they live with their grandmother. One day Kathleen put an audiocassette on the tape player and Marlys began singing along with the medicine man. "I didn't say anything," remarked Kathleen. "I acted like I didn't hear her. Theresa asked Marlys if she knew how to sing the old songs, and she said she did. She wasn't just making noises.

"Theresa is different. She calls herself a 'commotion lady' and she really is one. She can't sit down and do her homework by herself. She has to make a commotion and get everybody involved. Yet, we all know she can do it. The teachers are trying to show her how to work independently but she simply will not sit still."

Kathleen got up from the table to get drinking glasses for the girls, who were leaping and bounding into the house. "A real commotion lady," she added, handing Theresa a soft drink. "Get ready for supper," she instructed. "We're going to eat real soon." Marlys placed a small bouquet of wildflowers she had picked for her grandmother on the table. "OK," they chorused and skipped off to their room. Kathleen Kanseah watched them. Love filled her dimpled face and a smile broke out all over.

A few months later, Kathleen Kanseah lay in a hospital bed in Ruidoso, just north of the reservation. Her left hip had been replaced by one of modern medicine's prostheses. Pale but full of pep five days after surgery, she described what happened. "I heard a terrible noise outside," she said, "and went to see what was going on.[32] I left the two girls in the house. We were all alone. Well, the wind was blowing the barn door open and then banging it shut. I had a flashlight so I could see what I was doing when I closed the door tightly, but I fell over an old log that I knew was on the ground. That old log had been there forever, and I had stepped over it so many times before, but this time it got me. I fell sideways and I knew right away that something real bad had happened. Somehow I raised myself to my knees and then yelled for the girls. Theresa came outside and started crying right away when she saw I was hurt. 'Honey,' I said, 'don't worry about Grandma now. Just get me some blankets first.' I knew I was going into shock. She brought the blankets out of the house, and I put one on the ground and fell onto it and covered myself with the others. Then I told Theresa to call one of our cousins who lives nearby. Well, they came right away and called the ambulance. I was shaking and my teeth were chattering and I knew I was slipping away. My leg was numb. I looked up and the stars were so close I could practically touch them. Just as I felt myself going under, an aspen leaf came from somewhere and fell on my left shoulder. Then I knew I wasn't alone, and I got stronger right away. I told you that the old man Eugene Chihuahua predicted I'd have to be strong. He was so right."

Surgery on Mrs. Kanseah's broken hip was postponed for two days because the "parts" had to be found either in Albuquerque or El Paso and then shipped to Ruidoso. A week after the accident and five days post-op, Kathleen Kanseah amazed the medical staff by walking down the hall with the aid of a walker. Claiming to have no pain, she laughed aloud when told that her brother said she was getting ready to chase the men again. With her ear-to-ear grin filling the hospital corridor she countered, "Not me. I've got two girls home waiting for me and they need my help. I'm doing so well the doctor thinks I'll be discharged by the weekend. The girls will probably have a lot of homework to catch up on and I'll be right there to see that they do it. You know, last week Marlys got all twelve new spelling words right . . ."

Apache
Women
from
Oklahoma

THE SMALL-TOWN SETTING

To a desert dweller, the sight of ponds, lush green vegetation, and tall-grass pastures with fat cows are such a dramatic change that just being near the greenery is a minivacation. And so it felt on this trip to Oklahoma during one very hot week in early August 1989.

The drive from Albuquerque through eastern New Mexico towns led to speedy and smooth Texas ribbon roads and flatlands that were a marked change. Every now and then the hot and humid outside temperature interfered with the car's air conditioning, but the heat didn't bother us. Ahead of us in Anadarko, Oklahoma, was a week of hard work, coupled with anticipated enjoyment of all the events and festivities that were a part of Anadarko's annual American Indian Exposition. And certainly not incidental was the fulfillment of a longtime wish: an interview with the chairwoman of the Fort Sill Apache Tribe, Mrs. Mildred Imach Cleghorn.

Anadarko calls itself the Indian Capital of the Nation,[1] and throughout the year hosts a number of prime Native American events such as the Kiowa Black Leggins Ceremonial, the Great Southern Plains Rendezvous, and two events in August: the All-Indian Rodeo and the popular American Indian Exposition. During the exposition, numbers of tribes compete for national awards in the World Championship Fancy War Dance contest; tiny tots get dressed up in traditional tribal attire and win prizes for the best costume; the women hold a buckskin-and-cloth dance contest; greyhound and horse races are held every afternoon; and a judged art show and arts and crafts are exhibited inside one of the buildings on the Caddo County Fairgrounds. Unscheduled activities, needless to say, outnumber the events on the program, but nothing—absolutely nothing—can outdo the sight of talented male dancers, dressed in superb plumery, performing their tribe's traditional dances.

The resplendent Kiowas wear fanciful plumes and headpieces of multicolored feathers, have bells on their moccasins, and wear beaded headbands to hold back their long black hair. The irrepressible Comanches, dressed in their Northern Plains style, wear furs and feathers, heavy and dark, and paint a menacing black strip across their eyes. The quieter Sac and Fox wear dark blue skirts with red belts. Their hairpieces are porcupine quills sticking straight up from a band that travels from the forehead over the skull and down the back of the head toward the neck.

Indian Princesses from many tribes also participate in the exposition, chaperoned by their managers; they peek shyly out from under beaded tiaras or felt straps across their foreheads. In their hands they hold feathers wrapped together at the quills by fancy beadwork. Tribal directors are in traditional women's costumes of calico, solid colors, and beads. Other young women wear buckskin dresses, their fringes hanging close to the ground, with magnificent hide shawls covered with patterns in bright beadwork. Attending all of these Native Americans in their finery are drummers and singers, men whose voices have been trained in the music of their people. They sing the "Kiowa War Chant" and the "Apache War

Dance"; they pound their drums in ancient rhythms, making sounds that fill the air and float over the city of Anadarko.

Other, more permanent, attractions in the small city include the National Hall of Fame for Famous American Indians, the Southern Plains Indian Museum and Crafts Center, the Philomathic Pioneer Museum, the Delaware Tribal Museum, Indian City, USA, and a historic downtown where Geronimo, wearing a top hat, once drove an old car in the exposition parade.

August 1989 was also when the distinguished Apache chief Cochise was to be honored at the National Hall of Fame for Famous American Indians. A bronze bust of him, created by California sculptor Betty Butts, was to be dedicated and accepted by the Hall of Fame as part of a permanent exhibit in the "shrine dedicated to American Indians who have contributed to the molding of our American way of life."[2] Elbys Hugar, representing the entire family of Cochise, past and present, was an essential part of the ceremonies.

Founded February 1, 1952, the outdoor exhibit was conceived by Logan Billingsley of Katonah, New York, an employee of the U.S. Indian Service in Anadarko before Oklahoma's statehood. Unveiling ceremonies for the twenty-seven bronze sculptures now on exhibit have been held throughout the nation, but the busts are always sent to Anadarko to be enshrined. Included are such notable Native Americans as Massasoit, the revered chief of the Wampanoags, who greeted the Pilgrims when they landed in Massachusetts; Osceola, the Seminole war leader; Will Rogers, the famous American of Cherokee descent; Alice Brown Davis, a Seminole chief who was an outstanding leader in education and Christian culture among her people; Sacajawea, the Shoshoni woman who was the guide and interpreter for the Lewis and Clark expedition to the Pacific in 1805–1806; Quanah Parker, the most influential and prominent leader of the Comanches; Hiawatha, the Mohawk Indian that Longfellow wrote about; Hosteen Klah, a skilled Navajo medicine man; Pocahontas, a Powhatan woman who saved the life of Captain John Smith of Jamestown when she was only thirteen years old; and Geronimo, the brave and daring Apache leader.

Each year the week's festivities formally begin with a parade led by the

Indian of the Year, a prized designation made by the directors of the exposition. In 1989 the directors unanimously chose to award this honor to Mildred Imach Cleghorn because of her many activities on behalf of all Indian peoples. But before any of the formal activities began, the Mountain Spirit dancers, called the *Gah'e* by the Apache people, had come from the Mescalero Reservation in New Mexico to dance as part of their participation in the exposition and in honor of the presentation of the bust of Cochise.

Arrangements had been made for the *Gah'e* to dance on the night before the official ceremony in a special arbor at Indian City, USA—the only existing historic restoration of American dwellings and the Native American way of life. According to a publicity piece, "Truly authentic in every detail, the villages of Indian City, USA were planned by and constructed under the supervision of the Department of Anthropology, University of Oklahoma," and are a "living memorial to the American Indian."[3]

As the hour grew late that night, Indian people from many tribes brought their lightweight chairs to the dance arbor and set them up in a circle. The heat was oppressive, and the many adults fanned themselves steadily with handkerchiefs, newspapers, or anything else that was immediately available. Children didn't notice the weather. They were too busy chasing each other around the enclosure and making new friends.

Not too long after the Apache fire starters lighted the wood in the center of the grassy arena, a blazing fire roared a welcome to all visitors. Strangely, its heat wasn't even felt by many around the circle. The *Gah'e* were preparing themselves in a special tepee just down a slight incline from the dance grounds. Eventually, everyone heard the tinkle of their bells and the swish of their long yellow buckskin skirts. They came out of the dark trees directly opposite the fire, sounding their spiritual "coo" and shuffling up to the burning logs. In a straight line, the *Gah'e* danced toward the fire, waved their symbolic wands at it, and retreated. They approached the fire from another direction and repeated their advances until the four directions had been addressed. Framed by the blazing logs' light and accompanied by male singers and drummers and women in shawls who had come forward out of the crowd, the *Gah'e* were an extraordinary sight. When they had blessed the fire, the *Gah'e* continued their sacred rituals.

Apache women wearing fringed shawls joined their sisters already in the arena and danced in a clockwise circle, surrounding the spirit dancers. In groups of two, three, four, or more, they moved their feet in short half steps and turned their shoulders toward the fire in time with the drumbeat and the songs of the Apache men. Lighted only by flames, the Apache women reaffirmed and reinforced their ancient ritual, as their mothers, grandmothers, and great-grandmothers had done before them. In the orange brown firelight, many of the women appeared to be beautiful illusions floating before the watchful eyes of the mesmerized observers, all of whom could be easily hypnotized by the music, the *Gah'e*, the fire, and the heavy male voices. Young boys added to the mystique by sitting on the ground and, with thick sticks in their hands, slapping a hide placed on the earth in front of the singers and drummers. Every movement had meaning, every step around the fire had a history, every song or chant had its origin in the Apache spirit world. And every Apache woman in the circle danced to honor their ages-old faith and traditions.

Coming around the circle from the north, an elegant-looking Apache woman moved slowly and with great purpose. Readily visible because of her height, although second in a short line of women, Mildred Imach Cleghorn turned her body left and then right as her feet followed the rhythm of the Indian drums. By dancing with the *Gah'e*, the Fort Sill Apache tribal chairwoman paid her personal tribute to the spiritual legacy of the Apaches. Wrapped in a fringed blue shawl, her gray hair highlighted by the fire, Mildred Cleghorn turned her face to the fire, her thoughts far away. Beautiful and straight as an arrow, she closely followed the leader, her cousin Kathleen Kanseah. The Apache women knew in their bones when to stop and when to start up again, when to turn around and say hello to others who had joined their line, and when to pull the shawl closer around. Mrs. Cleghorn has been doing this dance for a long, long time. At eighty years of age, she has participated in hundreds of dances. During this venerable ritual and at all other times, this unique Apache woman has constantly held the fire and the faith of her people in her heart. It shows in her beauty. It shows in her vigor. It shows in her intelligence. It shows in her eyes. Without a doubt, Mildred Cleghorn carries the pride and passion of the Apache people.

What is not obvious, however, is her personal history. Mildred Imach Cleghorn was born into captivity in 1910 and, as an Apache child, was a U.S. prisoner of war at Fort Sill, Oklahoma. Released in 1914, she remembers riding across the countryside with her mother and father and coming down a hill to take up residence in a three-room house built on property the government had given her family. She still lives on that allotment, carved from Comanche lands, about twenty miles north of Fort Sill.

Fort Sill is today a busy artillery post with about sixty thousand men and women on active duty within its boundaries. The fort's history is briefly summarized in a pamphlet:

> Fort Sill was founded by General Philip H. Sheridan on January 8, 1869, during a winter campaign against the South Plains tribes. The Post was constructed by the black troopers of the 9th and 10th U.S. Cavalry, the famed "Buffalo Soldiers." Since 1911 Fort Sill has been the home of the U.S. Army Field Artillery Center and School. On the broad firing ranges of its 94,000-acre military reservation, generations of Field Artillerymen have learned the art of tube, missile, and aerial gunnery as defenders of the free world.[4]

No mention is made of the fort's role in the imprisonment of the Apache people. An activity such as the confinement of an entire group for so long a period of time (twenty-seven years for those who went to the Mescalero Reservation in New Mexico, and twenty-eight years for those who chose to remain in Oklahoma after release) constitutes a major segment of the fort's early history and, as such, deserves mention. But the army has, understandably, chosen to not publicize its participation in this shameful episode in the history of our nation.

The contemporary Fort Sill bustles and snaps with efficiency, from the squeaky-clean young man in uniform at the gate who is overly polite and exceedingly helpful, to an officer in camouflage fatigues who explains the rules of the commissary, to a female enlistee who points the way to the bathroom. Automobile and army vehicle drivers on the post are courteous and wait at stop signs as an unsure stranger drives along slowly. Following the signs to Geronimo's grave, the visitor leaves the carefully manicured grounds and reaches a roadway with overgrown bushes on both sides. The last indicator before the cemetery points to the right, but it is a different type of guide—a square metal sign anchored in concrete and painted carefully in Fort Sill's colors alerting everyone to the "landfill and rubble pit." An arrow on the sign points the way to the Apache cemetery.

At the cemetery itself is another marker naming some of those buried just a few feet away:

> The roll call of chiefs, warriors, Army scouts and families buried here include the most famous names in Apache history: Geronimo, whose daring band performed deeds unmatched since the days of Captain Kidd [*Captain Kidd?*]; Chief Loco of the Warm Springs, who stood for peace; Chief Nana, the original desert fox; Chief Chihuahua, of the Chiricahuas; and sons and grandsons of Mangus Colorados [*sic*], Victorio, Naiche, Cochise, and Juh and of such noted scouts as Kaahteney, Chatto, Kayitah, and Martine. Here also lie twelve of the fifty Apaches who were U.S. soldiers and scouts at Ft. Sill. Linked with these men in the Indian wars was a legion of Army greats— General [*sic*] Crook, Miles, Howard, Crawford, Gatewood, Lawton, Grierson, and Leonard Wood.
>
> This cemetery on Beef Creek was established in 1894 by General Scott. Related cemeteries are nearby—the Chief Chihuahua plot one-fourth mile north and the Bailtso plot just south across the road. Scouts Mangus and Dameah and white interpreter George Wrottan are buried in the Post Cemetery, Fort Sill, Oklahoma.[5]

The name of George Wratten, a man who was an important advocate for the Apache people during their years of imprisonment, is misspelled. According to Albert E. Wratten, George's son from a second marriage, the Apache interpreter was born in Sonoma, California, on January 31, 1865. He was of English background and had five siblings—three sisters and two brothers. For reasons of health, in late 1879 the family moved to Florence, Arizona Territory, where George quickly learned to speak Apache. By 1881, at the age of sixteen, he was officially a chief of scouts for the U.S. government. Because he had the confidence of the Apache people as their interpreter, Wratten was selected by Lieutenant Charles B. Gatewood to accompany him and two Indian scouts into Mexico to talk Geronimo and

Amy (left) and Blossom White, Fort Sill Apache daughters of George Wratten. (Courtesy of Fort Sill Museum, Fort Sill, Oklahoma, photograph no. P1501)

his warriors into surrendering. It was 1886 and Wratten was twenty-one years old. As a result of this experience, he was assigned to accompany the prisoners of war throughout the remainder of his life, first to Florida, then to Mount Vernon in Alabama, and finally to Fort Sill.

Wratten made several trips to Washington, D.C., on behalf of the Apache prisoners before he became too ill to continue as an advocate for the Apache people. He died at Fort Sill on June 23, 1912, and is buried in the post cemetery at Fort Sill; a big red boulder marks the spot.[6]

George Wratten dearly loved the Apache people, and he married a Chiricahua Apache woman, Nah-Goy-Yah-Kizn (the name means "tomboy" or "kids romping and kicking"),[7] known as Annie. She was the daughter of the older brother (name not recalled) of one of Geronimo's horse holders and apprentices, Lot Eyelash. An orphan, Annie had a varied history within the tribe and was quite an independent woman. She and George Wratten had two daughters, Amy (October 4, 1890–September 28, 1956) and Blossom (January 25, 1893–December 30, 1981). On January 17, 1913, Annie received severe burns in an accident and died the following morning of extensive capillary embolism.

In captivity, Amy Wratten married Richard Imach (1883–1948), a young, handsome Warm Springs Apache, whose Apache name was Ee-nah. Richard was the son of Go-lah-ah-tsa (her name means "did many things" or "does many things") and Clee-neh. About 1897, well before the marriage, Richard was sent to Carlisle Indian School in Pennsylvania from Fort Sill. He stayed the full three years and received what was, at that time, an extensive education for a prisoner of war. Richard and Amy Imach had two daughters, Mildred (born December 11, 1910), and Myrtle, who died as a baby.

A visit to the Apache cemetery at Fort Sill is an emotional experience. Often, names on the government markers are difficult to pronounce. Many deceased are described as "mother of . . ." or "aunt of . . ." or "sister of . . ." Other markers just list the words "Apache woman" under her name. One woman's epitaph reads simply "Clara's Aunt," with no other explanation.

On an August day, the quiet and solemnity of the burying ground was vulgarly interrupted by the whirring noise of a motorized grass cutter driven by a young soldier. Roaring around the cemetery, the machine's

Mildred (left) and Myrtle Imach.
(Courtesy of Fort Sill Museum, Fort Sill, Oklahoma, photograph no. 83.20.21)

blades snapped up plastic and silk flowers that had been laid on the graves by visiting relatives. The shredded remains were spit out by the machine and flew through the air, finally falling indiscriminately on other graves. The soldier, aware he was being watched, shrugged his shoulders and drove on. Once, he collided with a granite marker and had difficulty putting the grass cutter in reverse to back away. With a curse, he revved the engine and bolted backward. Cursing again, he drove on hurriedly through the narrow grass-covered corridors separating the rows of graves. An examination of the markers made it obvious that the mower had previously done quite a bit of damage. The names on some had been obliterated by deep scratches and scrapes.

When contacted about these circumstances, the superintendent of cemeteries at Fort Sill, a Comanche man who is a civilian employee, promised immediate attention. Most especially he was concerned about the sign announcing the presence of a landfill and rubble pit, and stated it would be removed.

Geronimo's grave, however, will probably always remain intact. He is buried under a pyramid of stones, cemented together, with a cement eagle perched atop the mound. Souvenir hunters have, in the past, stolen the eagle's head, scratched their names in the nameplate, and tried to remove the stones. It is well known that from time to time the cement eagle must be replaced, wholly or in part, and other small repairs must be made to the high pile of rocks. A simple nameplate, "Geronimo," is the only epitaph for a man whose fame as a warrior and as a medicine man will most likely never be forgotten.

Buried beside Geronimo are his last wife, Zi-yeh, and some of their children. Other members of the Geronimo family are buried nearby, including his beloved sister, Ishton, who was the wife of Chief Juh and mother of Asa Daklugie. To the left and slightly behind the mound is a single grave of someone named "Francisco," a man's name, but the marker identifies the deceased as a woman. This might be Francesca, the woman Geronimo admired so much and married because of her ability to overcome the many trials and tribulations she suffered.

In one section of the Fort Sill Apache Cemetery are the graves of some

Geronimo, circa 1906.
(Photo from H. Henrietta Stockel Collection)

of the Haozous family, but not Blossom Wratten, the sister of Amy, mother of Ruey Darrow, and aunt of Mildred Cleghorn. A local newspaper puts her place of burial at the Fairview Cemetery in Apache, Oklahoma.[8]

Blossom Wratten Haozous was born a prisoner of war in Alabama in 1893 and was moved with her family to Fort Sill one year later. Her first memory was "of the big tent town where the 341 Apaches were camped at Geronimo Springs after their arrival."[9] Later,

> The government just gave us little two-room houses with a breeze-way in the middle. The breezeway looked something like a narrow carport. We'd cook in one side and sleep in the other. If it was a big family, you used both rooms to eat, cook, and sleep in.[10]

Said Mrs. Haozous,

> He [her uncle] and his wife raised me and . . . my sister. She was older than I was . . . about three years older than me. My aunt used to cook out on the open fire. They [the government] gave them all nice big iron ranges, cookstoves. But she wasn't accustomed to cookin' on those. She'd rather cook outside. . . . In wintertime when it got too cold to cook outside, she used it [the stove]. Then it helped heat up the room, too.[11]

Mrs. Haozous recalled one of her earliest experiences—the Mountain Spirit dancers and the puberty ceremony.

> I saw my first dance there [at Fort Sill]. The one where the young lady comes into womanhood. They gave a feast and dance. I was so little, I don't remember much about it. I was a little bit frightened of the fire dancers when I first saw them. I never saw anything like that before. They never danced when we were in Alabama. Them dances they did in Arizona and New Mexico. When they [the Apaches] were prisoners of war in Florida and Alabama and those places, they didn't have those dances. Till they got settled in Fort Sill. Then they started them.
>
> At the time [of the puberty ceremony] they give a dance and give away stuff. At that time they gave out apples and oranges and candy and things that they got accustomed to using. They usually did that on the last day. It was a four-day affair. To this day they do that over in Mescalero, New Mexico. People just snatch-grabbed at it, grabbing stuff that was thrown out on the ground.
>
> On the first day they have some kind of a ceremony. They sing to

you and spread a big buckskin on the ground and then they place you on there on your stomach and they massage you. They do all kinds of things to you and then they pray for you. Then they let you get up. Then they put a basket of feathers and some kind of grass— it's eagle feathers and something that's supposed to be sacred. They put it in this woven Indian basket out toward the east and then they stand this girl up after they had massaged her and they give her a little shove. On the fourth time she gets her big shove, she runs around that basket and then comes back. They'd do that over and over four times.

. . . During those days when they're givin' you your dance, they put on your buckskin dress and you wear it the full four days. You're not allowed to drink water out of a cup. They used to give you a bamboo tube they would tie onto your dress and you'd drink with that. They said you weren't supposed to wash your face for four days.

. . . On the last day is when they throw out all that food for people to pick up. That was the giveaway to the crowd.[12]

As a young girl, Blossom Haozous played Indian baseball, rode horses, and went swimming with other children. She made dolls out of old rags and learned to do beadwork by watching her aunt. It was a time when Apache women gathered willow branches and empty tin cans from the soldiers. They wove sturdy baskets from the willow and decorated them with cone-shaped jingles made by cutting out tiny pieces of metal from the cans. No doubt Blossom Wratten watched the older women weave and line with pine pitch the jugs into which the water she hauled would be poured; she recalled having to walk a quarter of a mile to the village well. She had no chores actually connected with farming but did remember many things about farming, including the mules.

The army supplied them [the Apache people] with condemned mules. The men would go over and ask for a team, wagon, and plow and the soldiers would let them have it from the post. When they got through, they would take it back so somebody else could use it.

The condemned mules were still usable. The army just had no fur- ther use for them so they let the Apaches use them. They had a corral for those animals. They lent them out to the Indians to plow their gardens.

The army supplied the Indians with walking plows and walking cultivators, and all kinds of old-time things. They gave us rations every five days. They gave us fresh beef, coffee, sugar, and candles. Seems to me like they gave us *some* bacon at some point. When the Indians had a feast the army would give us a cow to butcher. I don't remember if it was one cow or two, but they did that for special occasions.

The whole tribe would come to the feasts. There were a few hundred of us. There was enough meat for a little piece for everybody. Most of the time they had a big place there where they did the cookin'. They usually boiled the meat or broiled it over the hot coals. They also had dried corn. They'd boil it with beef bones.[13]

Drying corn in those days was a simple procedure. The outer shucks were removed with just enough husk left on to protect the kernels from the fire. A pile of corncobs was placed in the fire, and when the time was right (Apache women knew instinctively when that was), the cobs were shoved out of the flames onto the ground where they cooled. After a while, the women cut the corn off the cob and spread the kernels on top of a canvas out in the hot sun. In the evening, the corn was brought indoors, and then returned outside the next day. When the kernels were dry, they were placed in a sack and the bag was hung on a wall of the house for storage. "They didn't have cupboards or built-in cabinets or anything like that," said Mrs. Haozous. "You just put 'em in bags and hung 'em around in the house. Everything you wanted to get out of your way, you hung on the walls."[14]

Mrs. Haozous was living with her aunt in one of the houses without storage facilities when she met her future husband, Sam Haozous, a former Apache warrior, athlete, and Indian scout.

My husband was related to her [the aunt] and he was single . . . his wife had died. He used to come there and visit. He'd bring meat or something for her to cook and she'd feed him. That's what got us acquainted. He used to come see her, then later he started comin' to see me . . . [my aunt] lived with us until she died . . . in my house.

They were married on February 12, 1910, at Fort Sill. Mrs. Haozous recalled,

> We moved into his house. He was an offspring of Mangas Coloradas. His uncle helped raise him and that's where he lived. He had sealed in his middle breezeway. Later he made a wall on the north side and screened in the south side and then put a floor in it. That made kind of an extra room there. It wasn't closed in on the south. It was just closed with a screen.[15]

Mr. Haozous was an army scout at Fort Sill and had varied duties. Some scouts rode fence, were overseers, or worked in the fields, barns, or wherever they were assigned by the army. In later years, Mr. Haozous was a truant officer, riding around the fort on horseback to collect the children who played hookey from school. He also broke horses and roped cattle for the military.

Blossom and Sam Haozous became the parents of five children: Ethelsu, Allan, Alfred, Ruey, and Peg. After the release of the Chiricahua people in 1913, the family made its home in Apache, Oklahoma, about twenty miles north of Fort Sill. When she was pregnant with her third child, Mrs. Haozous stayed with her sister because the doctor was nearer to Amy Wratten Imach's house, and also because Amy would help take care of the first two babies while Blossom awaited this birth.

All of her children have been successful, a quality Mrs. Haozous believed was the result of education. When the family was in need of money to educate their children, the Indian agency in Anadarko, Oklahoma,

> gave educational loans to the Indians—whoever wished to educate their children. We didn't make enough money on the farm to send everybody to college . . . we had to get some help some way. We paid it back. Every year when your crop came in you pay so much money back. We sold the crops and sent in the money. . . . You just sell it down here at the elevator . . . everybody hauled their wheat and corn or anything they raised down here at the elevator. They paid you

what the market price was . . . wheat and corn and cotton was our main crops.[16]

Blossom Haozous's commitment to education was lifelong, and not only regarding her own children. In October 1963, long after her children were out of school, Mrs. Haozous participated in an American Indian seminar at the Riverside Indian School auditorium in Anadarko, Oklahoma. She read a manuscript entitled "A Quarrel between Thunder and Wind," which is an Apache story, but what is unusual is that she read the tale in both English and Apache. It was reproduced bilingually in *The Chronicles of Oklahoma*:

A QUARREL BETWEEN THUNDER AND WIND

This happened a long time ago
when the earth was being made. The
Thunder and the Wind had a quarrel.

The Thunder and the Wind were to
work together as one, but they got angry
with one another. So they parted.

The Thunder spoke to the Wind. "I am
the only one that does good though you do
not help me."

So the Wind told the Thunder. "You are
the only one that does good, so now I will
leave you." The Wind went to the edge of
the earth.

Now, there was no wind. It was very
hot. The Thunder said, "I am not the only
one that does good." There was abundant rain
but it was still very hot.

There was no harvest. It was not good.
There was no wind. The Thunder did not feel

good about it. He stuck feathers in the ground
and looked, looked for the wind on the feathers.

"It is not right," said the Thunder.
Then he spoke to the Wind. "You are nowhere
and it is not good. There was no harvest and it
is very hot.

"Therefore, I beg you to return. Then we
will work together and there will be good
harvests," the Thunder pleaded.

So, the Wind came back to the Thunder.
Now, when it rains, the Thunder and the Wind
work together. They travel over the earth
together.[17]

In speaking of how life was while they were still at Fort Sill, Mrs. Haozous described the way the women made bread. "It was what people call
tortillas now," she said.

> They flatten it [the dough] out and cook it over the hot coals. They
> didn't have a grill to cook it on. They made a little rack and put
> live coals under it. You browned one side and then turned it over
> and browned the other. They made a rough rack out of bailin' wire
> mostly. Wove it back and forth and then put little legs on 'em or
> propped it on rocks to hold it up. The bread would rise a little bit
> and make bubbles. They'd have big baskets of bread like that to give
> out to the people with meat and corn, and sometimes they would
> use dried fruit like peaches. . . . We dried pumpkin, too. You cut the
> pumpkin open and dug out all the seeds and then you peeled it. . . .
> Then you start cuttin' around and just make a long string of it . . .
> then you drape 'em over a line . . . or branches and let 'em dry.[18]

After her marriage, she attended a group meeting in which a demonstration agent taught her how to can and do a lot more cooking. She first
canned green beans, and then corn.

We didn't have no pressure cookers and we just had to boil 'em in a big kettle. Jars and all. That's the way she taught us to can.

We just had fryers once a year during spring. When our fryers came in, why we killed 'em and we fried 'em like we were gonna eat them, then we put 'em in a jar and processed 'em. . . . She taught us how to can chicken. And beef the same way. We'd cook the beef, then put it in jars, put liquid in it, then processed it. . . . It's been years since I canned. . . . We still like our dried meat. I don't dry much anymore, but once in a while I get a piece of steak and tenderize it, beat it, then put it out to dry.[19]

Mrs. Haozous was a hardworking woman, a trait her aunt impressed upon her when she was a young woman.

[My aunt] taught me how to work. She said, "Don't be lazy." She said, "This is your best friend, your hands." She never knew a word of English but she taught us to be kind and to be good people. She was a real good mother to us. I guess we were kind of different because our father was white. George Wratten, the interpreter for the Indians. He lived among the Apaches ever since he was fifteen, I think he said. He learned the language and he stayed with 'em all the time and wherever they were taken as prisoners. He went with them.[20]

Blossom Wratten Haozous died on December 30, 1981, at the age of eighty-eight, long after her husband, Sam, had passed on back in December 1957. In tribute to his grandmother, Fort Sill Apache Tribal Historian Michael Darrow said,

She was a very powerful woman, but very reserved. She was intensely religious and involved with the church—the Apache Reformed Church in Apache, Oklahoma. As far as religion is concerned, there are people going around trying to foist their religion off on other people, but the way she did things was an example of how Christians should live.[21]

Blossom Haozous taught her grandson Michael how to do the beautiful beadwork of the Apache people, and she told him about basket weaving.

> Grandma said she used to make baskets when she was a little girl, but her aunt would prepare the materials for her and she would just weave them. She didn't know how to prepare the materials. Now there are other people in the tribe who make baskets, but some of the work has faded out over the years. I can look at some of the baskets that are in existence and figure out what sort of procedures and processes were used.
>
> Aunt Mil [Mildred Cleghorn] and I are the only tribal members who do traditional Fort Sill Apache–type beadwork, or pretty much anything else. And with the baskets, it's like the people who made them previously are not teaching their children or grandchildren.
>
> There are about four or five people who can still speak the language fairly well, and they're broken down into age division. People over a certain age are able to understand the language but they can't speak it, and people below that certain age can neither understand it nor speak it. I can get maybe one or two words every paragraph. Even if someone was to learn the language, there wouldn't be anyone else for them to speak to.

If there was no one in Apache, might there be someone in Mescalero? "Yes, but they talk funny," added Michael Darrow.[22]

The town of Apache, Oklahoma, in which the Haozous family lived and which has such meaning for so many of the Fort Sill Apache people, is located midway between Lawton to the south and Anadarko to the north. It resembles a peaceful, old-fashioned American prairie town, one that freezes hard and long in the winter when icy winds sweep the snow-packed streets, but flourishes and is lush all through spring and summer. Wild grasses grow high here, right up to the bellies of the grazing livestock. Water and rainfall are plentiful. Tall trees wave their leaves at travelers and others. Fields of hay are cut and baled, not in square blocks but in six-foot-high round rolls. No superhighway or turnpike disturbs this parcel of Oklahoma. A two-lane road takes everyone where they want to go—

everyone, that is, except certain unfortunate armadillos, victims of traffic accidents, lying dead in grotesque positions beside the road.

In one corner of Apache a grain elevator rises imposingly over the town, and just down the street an old red-brick bank building with a steeple on its roof still provides financial services to residents and houses a museum. Across the street, the municipal building, also red brick and with a steeple, has tall and narrow second-floor windows painted over with individual murals. A small café in the center of town offers hamburgers for less than two dollars and adds a dish of cole slaw for ten cents. One favorite topic of conversation among local customers is the power and potency of home-grown onions.

The bridge over Cache Creek is reinforced with heavy timbers on the roadbed, and its steel beams are decorated with graffiti telling the world that somebody loves somebody else. Unleaded gas is cheaper than regular, but why not? Parking, besides being allowed along both sides of the street, also includes a strip in the middle of the broad main boulevard where cars can face each other, nose to nose, while their owners run errands, pay bills, or shop. There are no traffic lights in Apache, not even at the only major intersection, where an amber light blinks caution and drivers obey without fussing. Watching the cars, a policeman greets passersby politely; one almost expects him to tip his hat.

Some homes in Apache have no street addresses, and their listing in the telephone book is simply "N. of town," or "S. of town." Many residences are large, rambling clapboard houses with verandas and slanted roofs, and have been settled for years along tree-lined, shady streets. It is easy to believe that each home has a colorful history, and if it could talk, would tell tales about this part of the American West that few have heard before.

Just beyond the center of the community, the Apache Reformed Church sits amid a grove of old, healthy trees. A smooth green lawn, very well tended, buffers the church building from street traffic. Behind and to the side of the church, Hospers Hall is utilized for activities such as quilting and youth group interests. The pastor, dressed in bib overalls on a week-day, takes time to inform visitors about the many services his church offers congregants, including Wednesday night Bible study and hymn singing. Mildred Cleghorn is a faithful parishioner, and on these nights raises her soprano voice to sing in praise of her God. Alongside the church's parking lot, a wooden prayer chapel in the shape of a tepee invites all comers to seek solace, serenity, and privacy to pray within its walls.

Here, in the pastoral surrounds of Apache, Oklahoma, those Chiricahua who in 1913 elected to remain in the area instead of going to Mescalero, New Mexico, received allotments of land from the federal government. But it was not without an incredible amount of bureaucratic infighting, one-upmanship, and political wheeling and dealing among competing interests that the Apache people were finally, at long last, relocated and set free.

> Congressional efforts to release the Apaches from their status as prisoners of war demonstrated that expediency rather than altruism governed the motives behind these endeavors; for in the game of whose interests would be furthered most, the Apache prisoners were naught but pawns,

reported one author who painstakingly researched the chronology of events related to freeing the Apaches from captivity at Fort Sill; his document is flabbergasting.[23]

One person intimately involved in the political machinations was Scott Ferris, a U.S. representative from the Fifth Congressional District of Oklahoma, which included the town of Lawton, very near to Fort Sill. Many Lawtonians derived their income from work at Fort Sill, so when it became known that a decision to close the military post and allot those lands to the Apache people for residences was pending, Representative Ferris went into action. His constituents were being threatened, so he wheeled and dealed in Washington, D.C., to prevent the closure of the fort. At the same time, U.S. senator Robert L. Owen of Oklahoma introduced legislation to provide allotments of land ranging in size from sixty to eighty acres of farmland in the general area of the fort to the Apache people.

Simultaneously, Judge Advocate General George B. Davis argued against alloting military lands at the fort to the Apaches because he believed the post should continue as an army reserve. Another governmental entity, the Board of Indian Commissioners, demanded that the Apaches receive no less than eighty acres at Fort Sill. The Indian Rights Association, a private group, campaigned on behalf of the Apaches, while a committee of Lawton's citizens organized to oppose any allotment of lands—on the fort's grounds or off—in their area. Eager to protect the government's interests, the secretary of war revealed that more than $1 million had been spent to establish the Field Artillery School of Fire on the grounds, and he wanted a return on his investment. The Apaches had to be located elsewhere, he stated. Ferris introduced legislation permitting the Apaches either to elect to move to Mescalero or to remain at Fort Sill, an idea that was well received because of the general belief that once certain Apaches were transferred to New Mexico, most everyone else would follow. There would then be no need for the allotments in the Fort Sill area.

Several Indian organizations offered amendments to this legislation, and the slow process of political compromise began. One amendment, preferred by the Indian Office, allowed the interior secretary to allot land only on the Mescalero Reservation or on the Fort Sill grounds, while the second advocated a third idea—those electing to stay in Oklahoma would be granted land outside the fort. Ferris liked the latter proposal and suggested that the government use the Kiowa and Comanche lands ceded by those tribes in 1897, a recommendation akin to Senator Owen's earlier proposal.

On May 10, 1912, U.S. senator Thomas P. Gore introduced legislation creating a commission to effect Indian removal from Fort Sill. This bill contained an appropriation of $250,000 for the purchase of allotments in Oklahoma "not to exceed eighty acres of farming land or one hundred and sixty acres of grazing land" for each individual Apache to be released and settled on the designated land.[24] This was still not satisfactory to many, and then the New Mexico congressional delegation jumped into the debate. U.S. senator Thomas B. Catron insisted that the Apaches should not be sent to New Mexico. He described, in lurid detail, some of the actions committed by the Apaches, and then stated his belief that, despite all the years of imprisonment and the fact that many of the original leaders and warriors were dead, the Apaches would once again cause trouble because there wasn't enough land in New Mexico to keep them occupied. He recommended that they remain at Fort Sill. The other New Mexico senator, Albert B. Fall, strongly agreed. It was no secret that he wanted the lands at Mescalero to be utilized as grazing pastures for the flocks of his constituents and political friends. John Turcheneske reported that vehement opposition to the removal of the Chiricahuas had its origins in Roswell, New Mexico, and, aided and abetted by Fall, was instigated solely by stockmen strongly determined to protect their leases and their profits on the Mescalero Reservation.[25]

These ranchers, calling themselves the Roswell, New Mexico, Commercial Club, circulated a petition demanding that the Apaches be kept in Oklahoma and that all the tillable lands at Mescalero be divided among the current residents, with the remaining lands to be turned into a national park.

Finally, after all the clamor and political skullduggery, the amendment alloting lands outside Fort Sill was adopted, as was the proposal to permit those Apaches desiring to relocate at Mescalero to do so. On April 4, 1913, the Apaches who decided to move to New Mexico were freed. It took another year of political posturing to release the Apaches who had chosen to remain in Oklahoma and farm on their allotments of 160 acres per person.

Two families—those of Richard Imach and Sam Haozous—were among the Chiricahua Apaches who stayed in Oklahoma. Today, Mildred Imach Cleghorn and Ruey Haozous Darrow carry on the traditions of their families while simultaneously participating actively in contemporary mainstream American society.

Mildred Imach Cleghorn

Uncle Sam doesn't follow through . . .

"No one got 160 acres," says Mildred Imach Cleghorn, the chairperson of the Fort Sill Apache Tribe.[26] "The closest they got was 158 acres and the least amount they got was 23. A majority received 80 acres apiece. My father got 80 acres, my mother got 80 acres, and I live right here on 50 acres. Yes, we were promised 160 acres apiece, but Uncle Sam doesn't follow through. . . . We in Oklahoma stayed [at Fort Sill] one year longer [than those who went to Mescalero]. Because we had to find a place to live. It was about 1923 that the last Apache got an allotment."

Mildred Cleghorn's brick house sits on her allotment, way back from the road, just outside town where the two-lane route bends toward Lawton. It is a large, modern home built on an angle to the road, deliberately, so that one side of the home faces east. Believe it or not, up to eighteen people can sleep there overnight. It has happened. A cedar tree in the front yard was planted by Mrs. Cleghorn when she retired from her full-time job. That was back in 1965. She went to the countryside, dug up a small sapling, and brought it home for planting, not sure whether it would live or die, but wanting to commemorate her retirement somehow. The tree now spreads its branches and offers shade to automobiles, people, and dogs—not necessarily in that order and not necessarily all at once. There is a basketball court not too far from the tree, in the backyard, and yes, the eighty-year-old Apache woman still plays the game regularly with her grandchildren and her cousins' grandchildren. (Last time she counted, she had fifty-six cousins.) Basketball is easier for her to play than the violin, which is what she did years ago. Now, she complains, her arthritis prohibits the rapid finger movements necessary to do justice to the instrument.

Near the basketball court, two dogs she calls Butch and Annie greet visitors and circle a strange car, sniffing at where it has been and deciding if they like the intrusion, or the intruders. Other dogs visit periodically, and sometimes four or five animals bark as guests dash for a far corner of the patio where an entryway might be located. The back door is open and

Mildred Imach Cleghorn.
(Photo by H. Henrietta Stockel)

a storm door is all that separates strangers from the warmth of Mrs. Cleghorn's hospitality. She is in the kitchen, fixing coffee, and opens the door with a smile. Despite the pleasant welcome, however, one does not feel at home immediately. There is a mystery about Mrs. Cleghorn, and it emanates from her persona, not in an unfriendly or frightening way but in a self-assured, self-controlled, commanding fashion. "She was remarkable as a younger woman, but now she is absolutely outstanding," said Polly Lewis Murphy, a longtime member of the Oklahoma Historical Society.[27]

This is indeed a woman who is in charge—of herself, of her home, of the things around her, and of the people she invites into her domain. After a few minutes' exposure to this 1989 Indian of the Year, it is easier to relax, breathe naturally, govern the swirl of inner emotions—to begin to feel comfortable with her. What is it about this magnificent-looking Apache woman that is so formidable, yet alluring? Perhaps her posture—ramrod straight and tall, about five feet ten inches in height. Or perhaps her gray/white/silver hair, pulled taut and then brought forward in a French knot, framing a golden brown Indian face much younger looking than its years. Or the softness of her voice, her articulate statements, her confident walk, her smile, her huge rimless eyeglasses that hide sad brown eyes, her silver rings and bracelets that match her hair, her long silver feather earrings, the sense of drama as she enters her large living room and casually waves her guests beyond a free-standing fireplace toward sectional sofas. Exactly. All of these things and one more: the woman's unusual, almost palpable, power. Wordlessly, Mildred Cleghorn communicates authority, an eloquent physical, emotional, and intellectual supremacy . . . undoubtedly bred in the bone. This is a woman who must be seen in person to be fully appreciated. Descriptions are inadequate. And there is more: once in her circle, she is virtually spellbinding. Truly, it is almost impossible to leave her presence without her permission. Still, when all the labels are pinned and all the words are applied, she remains elusive. Who is this woman really, and how did she become the leader of the Fort Sill Apache Tribe?

Mildred Imach Cleghorn was born to Amy Wratten and Richard Imach, Apache prisoners of war, at Fort Sill on December 11, 1910. She is today one of a dozen or less Apaches still living who were born into captivity. She makes no secret of her plight and feels no need to be cautious in her statements about the American government's treatment of the Apache people. "From day one until today, they have never kept their promise," Mrs. Cleghorn declared. "As Indian people, we didn't need black and white to keep a promise. All we needed was your word. We didn't have to write it down. We believed them because that was our way of life. The army told Geronimo "two years," that he would be back home in two years. He believed. He never did come back. You know, Geronimo surrendered so the Apache people would not be annihilated. There's two sides to the man. One time he came home and found his family slaughtered and lying all over the ground. Bodies everywhere. Well, there you have a feeling, you know how much hurt and loss he suffered. His whole immediate family was killed by Mexicans, and that's awfully hard. When we lose one, it's bad enough, but to lose the entire family, your mother, your wife, your three children . . ."

No, neither Geronimo nor his family ever did return home to his be-loved Arizona, not even in death. In the Fort Sill Cemetery he and his loved ones rest not far from Mildred Cleghorn's grandmother and various kin. But his burial place and his bones might have been disturbed some years back if the result of a controversy among Apache peoples had been different.

Two Apache leaders in Arizona wanted Geronimo's remains returned to their area. They believed that only in this way would the spirit of their famous leader be honored. These men, at the time chairmen of the San Carlos and White Mountain Apache groups, objected to Geronimo's body lying in a white man's fort. The proposal offended the Mescalero Apaches, who cited Apache law that prohibits disturbing gravesites, and Mildred Cleghorn, by then already chairperson of the Fort Sill Apache Tribe, agreed. "Geronimo was our leader," she said. "He is buried at Fort Sill and his grave should not be disturbed. As far as I'm concerned . . . we need to respect the family's wishes."[28] This extraordinary situation produced a swirl of statements by Apaches in Arizona, New Mexico, and Oklahoma, as well as hard feelings because of allegations and accusations that accompanied the circumstances. When the issue was finally resolved, Geronimo remained at Fort Sill, and the rebuilding of good relationships began.

As Mrs. Cleghorn looks at archival photographs of Geronimo and other

Marianetta, wife of Geronimo. (Courtesy of Smithsonian Institution, National Anthropological Archives, negative no. 29,778)

Apaches, men and women, and her eyes fill with tears. Easily touched and moved by the circumstances her forebears suffered, both while trying to stay free and while prisoners of war, she has few memories herself of how life was in captivity. But there was one incident in particular . . . "When children needed someone," she said, "my mother always took them in. She took a cousin of mine, his mother had died, and was helping to raise him. We were small, so small that we could fit into a gunny sack. I remember him sitting looking at me and we were crying [inside the gunny sack]. My mother punished us because we set the barn on fire. Later, I could never get her to admit she did that, or even say yes or no. She just said, "Oh, I wouldn't do that."

The next memory Mildred Cleghorn carries is of the day her family was released from the prison at Fort Sill. "I remember coming over the hill, right here," she waved, "and we had a three-room house below the hill where the one is now. We were in a big wagon with a team of horses. My father pointed to it and said, "Now this is home. This is where we're going to live from now on." And she still lives there, on the fifty acres her father gave her from his total allotment.

Mrs. Cleghorn attended public school in Apache, Oklahoma, and then went to the popular Indian school known as Haskell Institute in Lawrence, Kansas. "During the Depression I either went to school at Haskell or didn't go to school at all," she said. "My mother had gone to boarding school and she said, "I don't want any child of mine going to a boarding school." I just begged to go to school because, having gone to public school in Apache, I didn't know any of the Indian children. When we went to Indian gatherings, I didn't know anyone. I was always alone and I wanted to know someone. So, when I begged my mother to let me go to Haskell, and she agreed, she said, "Now, the minute you get lonesome you come right home. You let me know and you can come right home." I promised her that I'd do that, but I didn't. I got so lonesome that I thought I'd die, but I wouldn't tell her that. I stayed and by the end of October, why, you couldn't drive me away."

Mrs. Cleghorn graduated from Haskell Business School and worked for the Bureau of Indian Affairs in Kansas until 1937. It was office work, something that was strange to her, and it didn't take her long to learn that the four walls couldn't contain her spirit. "I didn't like it," she said. "I had always wanted to be an extension agent, working with families on the reservation is what I always wanted to do in Indian work. I went back to college then in 1937 and got my degree in home economics in 1941. I taught school then for a year and a half. One of the requirements was that I had to teach for two years, but they let me go early because there was a job opening. They asked me if I would take it and I said sure."

That job was in the Riverside School, an Indian educational facility less than fifty miles from Apache, Oklahoma. "We had a cottage department at Riverside," she remembered. "One of the most wonderful opportunities our Indian children ever had was being in cottages because we created a home life situation. There were twenty-two students, eleven boys and eleven girls from all tribes. Navajos, people from the North, and everywhere," she said. "It was just one big family and each child had their work to do. So, they learned how to keep house, how to cook, how to do the laundry, how to do everything. The students polished the furniture, swept the floors, and polished the floors. Then we had study hours. I think it was the most wonderful thing that could ever have happened. Today I get graduation notices from the grandchildren of the children I taught, which is amazing to me. I have never seen these people in the flesh, but I have their pictures. They have jobs that are responsible, and you can see the difference."

While working in the Pawnee Indian area of Kansas, Mrs. Cleghorn met her future husband. Much later, they were married on the Mescalero Apache Reservation. "My cousin Kathleen Kanseah and I had a double wedding in New Mexico," she recalled. "Kathleen got married in the Catholic church in the morning and I got married in the Reformed church in the afternoon. Her father, who was my favorite male cousin at the time, gave me away because my own father had died." Mildred and Bill Cleghorn had no children of their own, but there is one adopted daughter, Penny, who now has several children.

For the last ten years, Mildred Cleghorn has headed the Fort Sill Apache Tribe, a group of approximately 335 enrolled individuals. "There are very few of us, but we're still here," she said. "The government recognizes one-quarter blood quantum to be an enrollee in most tribes, but if we went to one-quarter, we wouldn't be 335 Apaches. Our blood quantum is one-eighth." She attributes this unusual situation to marriages outside the tribe to Comanche, Kiowa, and other Native Americans, as well as to Anglos. By not living on a reservation, the members of this tribe are more accultur-ated and participate in the mainstream society more than do their cousins at Mescalero. Even their tribal administration buildings differ.

The Apache Tribal Complex is located north of the town of Apache. A green-and-white highway sign on the right side of the road is the only alert a driver has that the tribal offices are near. Shortly after seeing the sign, the building rises on the left, following the crest of a hillock, not too far back from the road. These offices, modern in construction style, have a parking lot in front of the structure and an informal parking lot behind the complex. Dance grounds for the *Gah'e* are a few dozen yards away. A very large bronze sculpture of a Chiricahua family by noted Chiricahua Apache sculptor Allan Houser faces the morning sun. Mr. Houser is quite probably the most eminent American Indian sculptor working today, but he is also Mildred Cleghorn's cousin, Ruey Darrow's brother, Blossom Haozous's son, and the first Apache born in freedom.

"The farm was all we had," said Mr. Houser, speaking of his youth in Apache, Oklahoma.

> I credit my mother and dad for managing to feed us, especially dur-ing the Depression. The government allowed us rations of cornmeal flour. We had a few horses, hogs and chickens. We always exchanged garden produce with neighbors. Most of the Indians we knew then just about gave up. Even the Anglos were hurting and if it was hard for them, you know it was bad for the Indians. . . . I like to work. I worked in the cotton fields. During wheat harvest I'd saddle up a little horse and carry water for the workers. We used burlap wrapped around the water jugs to keep them cold. I guess I was around eight or ten at the time.
>
> We all got to go to grade school, but I had to drop out of high school to help with the farm. I was the oldest, and close to my dad. We farmed and played baseball together. He coached the ball team. We traveled around and had a lot of fun with it. I was doing things I

liked during my high school–age years—didn't care much for school, let's put it that way. I liked the freedom of working and helping.

But I was thinking, too, about what the future would hold. I thought of going into the cattle business. By the time I went back to finish school, I was nineteen and overage for the school near home. All the kids seemed young. Instead, I went to the old Indian School in Santa Fe, the one founded by Dorothy Dunn. It was the only art school an Indian could afford to go to in those days, because it was free.[29]

Mr. Houser remembers the stories his parents told him about what it was like when they were imprisoned. He remembers the oldest members of the tribe who wept when his father sang of the sufferings they had endured. To this day, he carries his Apache flute in a deerskin pouch made by his mother and cherishes the bow and painted quiver fashioned by his father. At the opening of his exhibit at Santa Fe's Wheelwright Museum in May 1984, Mr. Houser played that flute after delighting art patrons by announcing that the Indian music he was about to play had been played by his father to serenade his mother during their courtship.

Mr. Houser's Apache sculptures have been exhibited throughout the United States and in Europe. His work is included in the British Royal Collection and in such institutions as the Heard Museum in Phoenix, the Wheelwright and New Mexico Fine Arts museums in Santa Fe, and in private collections worldwide. His commissions include murals for the Department of the Interior Building in Washington, D.C.

While his credentials are indeed impressive—a Guggenheim Fellowship, the French government's Palmes de Académiques, the Philbrook Art Center Waite Phillip Trophy, the 1980 New Mexico Governor's Award for Excellence in the Arts, television appearances, an entry in *Who's Who in American Art*, and many others—Mr. Houser's philosophy is simple: "There are no limits as to ancestry or background in the making of an artist or in the appreciation of his work."[30] He believes this very deeply, and his work reinforces his belief. A massive seven-foot-high bronze sculpture, titled *Offering of the Sacred Pipe*, stands at the U.S. mission to the United Nations in New York City.

Mr. Houser's huge sculpture of a Chiricahua family faces the door into the tribal complex at Apache. Entry takes a visitor into a brightly lighted corridor with rooms off to one side. Mildred Cleghorn's unpretentious office is small and located in the middle of the group of rooms. It contains, along with the usual nondescript office furniture, her personal memorabilia and many references to Geronimo, both in print and in posters, hanging on the walls. Several plaques and awards decorate the room, along with photos of herself and others taken in Arizona when she and other Chiricahuas retraced the same routes their ancestors traveled more than one hundred years ago. She conducts the Fort Sill Apache Tribe's business from this office but is reluctant to go into much detail about her daily activities. "As chairperson, most of the time I spend reading," she commented. "I get so much literature. To keep up with things, I have to go to meetings and do a lot of reading. But mainly, what I want to do with the tribe is to preserve what culture we have, preserve our language, and learn more about our own people and history." Tears come into her eyes.

"I get very emotional about these things because I grew up on the stories," she said. "My father was a child when he was taken prisoner, so he didn't remember too many of the activities that went on. But my uncle used to tell us about it because he was older and was also involved in the warfare. He used to have to take care of the Apaches' horses. He would tell us the stories his people told him of what they saw, and then he would tell us what he saw. All of us in my generation just grew up on those stories, and we knew the Apaches always wanted to go back to Arizona.

"Not too long ago," she said, [referring to the Arizona trip], "we descendants went back to Fort Bowie and the surroundings on the centennial date of Geronimo's surrender—the one hundredth anniversary. We were just thrilled to death.

"I have traveled a highway in Arizona, year after year, visiting relatives in that part of the country, being right there where my people were, or near there, going through Apache country and never visiting. Then, in 1986, we went to Skeleton Canyon and stood where the old ones stood, camped where they camped, prayed where they prayed, and we completed the circle. That's the way we felt. We completed the circle."

The trip made by the Chiricahua descendants to the homeland of their ancestors September 4–7 1986, was a journey of sadness and honor. A century ago, on September 4, 1886, Geronimo and his band of seventeen warriors, fourteen women, and six children had surrendered to U.S. Army general Nelson A. Miles in Skeleton Canyon, deep in the Arizona desert. This small group had kept the soldiers, their weapons, and their military strategy off balance for five years.

During the four scheduled days of the journey, the descendants commemorated, but did not celebrate, this event. More than a year of planning by representatives from the Arizona Historical Society, the National Park Service, and the Apache tribes was necessary to make it happen. The commemoration took place in the small town of Bowie, at the nearby Fort Bowie National Historic Site, and in the Arizona desert. The formal ceremonies included reading a proclamation issued by the governor's office, a memorial cavalry ride over the sixty-five-mile route taken by General Miles's party, traditional Chiricahua Apache war, social, and Mountain Spirit dances, and various speakers presenting addresses such as "Apache History," "The Apache Experience," and "The Geronimo Campaign, an Overview." At Fort Bowie itself a flag ceremony was held, followed by recognition of the former Chiricahua Apache prisoners of war and an address by Mildred Cleghorn, which she entitled "The Fort Sill Experience." After other formalities, Chiricahua Apache music was presented by Fort Sill Apache tribal members. A benediction closed the entire proceedings.[31]

A commemoration of this historic event was also held on the Mescalero Reservation in New Mexico. The descendants prayed, danced, sang, and ate traditional Apache food to honor their ancestors. The *Gah'e* danced in the darkness around a roaring fire, and "sparks flew on gusts of wind and the smoke swirled to the sky as the Apaches danced and cried out in soft pulsating tones, reaching toward the heavens to invoke the spirits of the mountain gods."[32]

Lena Carr, a Navajo filmmaker, produced a documentary film that chronicled the Arizona portion of the commemoration. Entitled *Geronimo and the Apache Resistance*, the documentary was shown in New Mexico on public television on Thanksgiving evening 1988. Mrs. Edna Comanche, an eighty-six-year-old former Chiricahua prisoner of war who is a descendant of Eugene Chihuahua, got an advance look at the film. She commented, "I got a big scar right here," and lifted a hand from beneath a blue shawl to point to her arm. "Every time I got examined for school, I got vaccinated by a soldier . . . it hurt me."[33] Katherine Kenoi, an eighty-year-old former Chiricahua prisoner of war who lives at Mescalero, said, "My father, he didn't like to talk about Geronimo. He didn't want to remember anything about it."[34] Said Wendell Chino, chairman of the Mescalero Apache Tribe,

> Our history has been tragic and full of injustices that were forced upon our people. But they were strong and their strength of character and that attitude is what saw them through. . . . They said Geronimo engaged in guerilla warfare. A guerilla acts alone. You don't act alone when you have the blessing of your leadership.[35]

As Lena Carr was filming, the group of descendants placed U.S. flags on the Fort Sill Cemetery graves of Geronimo and the Apache chiefs Nana, Chihuahua, Loco, and Mangus. A flower wreath was laid at the grave of George Wratten, Mildred Cleghorn's grandfather, and then everyone sang Apache religious songs. One of the singers was Mildred Cleghorn, who later said that Geronimo should be remembered as a man who tried to save his homeland. "There are people in trouble now with the land who are being chased off it," she reminded listeners, "and who can empathize with us. If you stop to think about it, nobody wants to be chased off their land. Ask an Iowa farmer who's been foreclosed. They aren't standing by and letting someone take it."[36]

Lena Carr received a portion of her funding from the National Endowment for the Humanities, a $10,000 grant from the New Mexico Arts Division, an $8,000 grant from the New Mexico Endowment for the Arts, and a $10,000 grant from KAET-TV, a public broadcasting station in Tempe, Arizona. Through a reference from KAET-TV, she contacted Peace River Productions, a company headquartered in Cambridge, Massachusetts, that has a history of producing Indian-related features. That company contacted WGBH-TV in Boston, which was putting together the "American Experience" series, and Ms. Carr's concept was accepted. "I promised the Apaches we interviewed that Geronimo's story would be told from their perspective, not from the viewpoint of the whites," she said.

When I saw some of the film's early cuts, I realized that this hadn't been done. So I fought very hard to keep my promises. I felt as if my integrity depended on keeping my word to the Apache people and in the final editing, it is clear that I have. . . .

The Indian people must stand up for themselves, since they know that media representations of them are so stereotypical. They cannot wait around for the white film establishment to come around to their way of thinking—they must obtain their own funding and make their own films. It is up to the Indians to change the whole image of Native Americans on film.

Native Americans tend to be passive," she said, "but it's time for them to realize that if they don't preserve their own cultures, no one will do it for them. Writing books, singing songs, producing art like paintings and pottery and weaving—these are all ways to preserve the culture for the future. Filmmaking is another way.

Many Indian people are afraid of "non-traditional" arts, and movies and TV seem strange to them. But these are the art forms of the time. If Native Americans don't realize how important these medias are, they are going to be left behind without a trace.[37]

In discussing the film, Mildred Cleghorn commented, "We had an opportunity to say some of the things we've felt all of our lives. I don't think people know what really happened and they can't imagine it today. I'm an Apache prisoner of war and I'm still living. It sounds like history but, really, I don't feel like I'm history yet."

Because of all she has heard, all she has seen, and all she has experienced, Mildred Cleghorn is in an extraordinary position to comment upon history, even though, no, she isn't history herself. How does she feel about what happened to her forebears? "Well, I guess I've accepted it to a certain extent, but then again, I haven't. I still feel a personal loss. I can't speak my language today. I can understand it, yes, but we've lost it here in Oklahoma, and we've lost a lot of the good things. I try to live a Christian life, be a good Christian. I study the Bible like you do each day if you're a Christian."

Mrs. Cleghorn has served as an elder in the Reformed Church of America at Apache, Oklahoma, for the last fifteen years and represents the government of the church at the American Indian Council Committee, a group of six tribes under the umbrella of the church. Also, she sits on the General Program Council, one of the top organizations within the Reformed Church of America.

"I don't want to give the wrong impression," she said, "but the symbolism we have in the Apache tribe is the same symbolism that Christ has in the Bible. For example, fire. In our way, fire is very important. You notice the fire when we dance, when the Mountain Spirit dancers, the *Gah'e*, dance around the fire. Well, the Holy Spirit came down to the fire, too."

Although the generally understood image of the Apache people is not that of a particularly religious group, Mrs. Cleghorn continued to cite parallels. "They went up into the mountains, the high places, and Moses did that," she said. "They went into the high places to fast and pray, and they got a message. Moses got a message. That's why I say it's amazing how our people relate to the biblical standards of Christian religion, the symbolism I was mentioning before. Like the fire and the pollen. You can't get a flower or growth without pollen. Pollen to us represents fertility, and we color our clothes with yellow. That's why yellow is such a predominant color among our Apache people. There are so many beautiful things about our Indian people, our Indian way, that I hope we shall never lose.

"Also, we're taught to share in the Apache way," she added. "Well, there in the book of Matthew it tells you. The birds and the bees don't worry about what they're going to eat tomorrow, and that's the way our Indian people are. Today is when you live. So, you do what you can today to help other people, to share."

Mrs. Cleghorn leaned forward and took a sip of coffee. She held the cup, minus its saucer, in the palm of her left hand and turned it in a small circle with her right hand. She seemed lost in thought. "Then they say that we don't have any outstanding people that really get way ahead of everybody else," she remarked. "Well, yes, there are very few Apache 'up there' because after a certain level, you have to stick your neck out. Then you become more selfish and forget about others. You don't want that."

She relaxed a little and chuckled at something she was about to say. "One thing the white man jokes about is Indian time. Time means nothing to us, and it becomes amusing the way people break their necks when people say two o'clock, for instance. If you're going to an Indian affair, you're going to sit and wait a long time if you get there right at two o'clock. This is one thing we're having much difficulty with today. But if the Indians tell you they're coming, they might not be right on the dot, but . . . And that's one of the things all of us have to break. We have to learn that's not the way. It'll just take time," she laughed. "You all just have to be patient and wait a while."

While not exactly an Anglo cultural attribute, patience has always been one of the hallmarks of the Apache culture. During the earliest days of pursuit by the American army, the Apaches waited out the troops by hiding behind boulders and bushes, in arroyos, and in strongholds where they camouflaged themselves by wearing turbans of leaves and branches. Only when the danger passed did they emerge from their refuges and continue on their way. Apache women were patient when searching for foodstuffs, often having to walk many miles to fill a small hide sack with only a day's nourishment. And in discussions with Apache people, patience is still the rule. Many eager conversants have pushed a topic too far too fast, only to be met with stony silence from the Apache side. "In good time" is a rule of thumb in attempting to communicate with the Apache folks. In good time.

Of course, many of today's Apache youth don't subscribe to the doctrine of patience because they have been exposed to acculturation and want to move into the mainstream. Many have married out of the tribe, moved away, and ceased to observe the traditional rituals and customs. Too, there are only about a dozen former prisoners of war still alive, and they are aging rapidly. What will happen, then? Is it possible that the young people will change their current paths and return to tradition? "Well, maybe," said Mrs. Cleghorn. "It just thrills my heart when I get a letter from a young person. One young man who went to Dartmouth University wrote me that he had never seen us or our area of the country, but he had heard of us from his father and grandfather. Both of those gentlemen had gone to Carlisle Indian School and never came back home. Anyway, this young man wanted to come to Oklahoma so he could be near his people. He had heard his grandfather tell these stories and he wanted to get acquainted with the tribal members. So, he transferred and became a student at Oklahoma State University and came to our tribal meetings. Then he went to Santa Fe to the Indian Art Institute to absorb some more Indian culture, and he hopes to be a portrait artist in New York."

It is doubtful that the young man Mrs. Cleghorn holds in high esteem will ever be able to know or participate in certain activities that were once commonplace within the Apache culture, such as tanning a hide. This is an incredibly slow undertaking that begins with the removal of the hide from the animal, a task Apache women performed routinely not so long ago. The hide was soaked and then staked to the ground before the laborious chore of tanning began. Bones or stones were favorite instruments because they were easily held in one hand. Patiently, forcefully, the women scraped the fur off the hide, inch by inch, to the accompaniment of a nauseating odor and hundreds of flies. "I've only tanned one buckskin," said Mrs. Cleghorn, "and that was my first and last. At Whitetail in New Mexico, my aunt Gertrude Smith was tanning and I said I wanted to help, so she let me. When you start, you can't stop. You have to keep going. If you want to have a nice soft hide, you can't let it get dry. You have to work it dry. That's the old way. I haven't tanned or seen anyone tan hides for years, so I don't know if anyone still does it the old way today. It's hard work, but I know they have all kinds of new soaps now that cut down the time. Good riddance to the hand tanning, but if you could get the same quality of tanning in a modern version that was done by hand, it would be wonderful. The old tanning way took both sides of the skin into consideration, and it produced very soft leather. On the hides I've seen commercially tanned today, only one side is usable for what we want. Commercially tanned hides are not the same."

Mentioning some of the other ways that are no longer observed by the Fort Sill Apache Tribe's members, Mrs. Cleghorn surprisingly cites the puberty ceremony. Although Dorothy Naiche, the granddaughter of Cochise and the daughter of Naiche, made Mrs. Cleghorn's puberty dress, there was no ceremony in which to wear it. "Here in Oklahoma, we never had them," she said, referring to [the puberty rites]. "We didn't have anyone here to do the ceremony." She lowered her eyes. "I definitely feel I lost something. Definitely. And I don't think it will ever come back. It's gone for good."

However, in a manner typical of an Apache woman leader, Mildred Cleghorn has not stood idly by while aspects of the culture slipped away. In response to the challenge of preserving at least one important element—traditional clothing—she makes Apache dolls that have been widely praised for their authenticity. "I always played with dolls," she said smiling. "I even still have one dressed in buckskin that my mother made for me. When I was working at my job in Horton, Kansas, far away from Apache people, I joined a church organization there. It was a fellowship, a guild. One night they asked me to tell them about the work I did. At that time I was working with four different tribes, and even though the church people had lived there all their lives, they knew very little about Indians.

"They thought, as many people do, that we all did things alike, and I wondered how I could show them that we're so different from one another. Well, by their clothes, that's how; the women especially. There's not much difference in Indian men's clothes, but with the women, their dresses were entirely different. So, I chose to use women as an illustration and I said, 'Just look. Look at their clothes. These women are just as different as their clothes are.' To start with, making doll clothes was just a hobby. I made clothes for four dolls, and then I decided to make dolls to represent all the tribes I work with. That's still my ambition. I have forty dolls out of an anticipated seventy-two."

Several museums have purchased the dolls. There is a doll at the Southern Plains Museum in Anadarko, Oklahoma, and others at Ponca City and Duncan, Oklahoma. Six dolls are exhibited in the Future Homemakers Club of America's building in Washington, D.C., representing the state of Oklahoma. Then too, the dolls have been shown at the Smithsonian Institution twice, at various folklore festivals in the nation, in the Children's Museum in Indianapolis, and there are four dolls in a continually traveling exhibit. Most of the time the dolls are dressed in camp dresses that are made of cloth and follow a distinct pattern. "If you look at the buckskin dresses," said Mrs. Cleghorn, "they're so similar that you can't just look and see a difference. But in the cloth dress, there is a definite difference in the patterns tribes used. A lot of times the people who want the doll tell me to use trade cloth. Many of the northern dolls are dressed in trade cloth."

Before beginning a costume, Mrs. Cleghorn thoroughly researches a tribe's clothing habits. "When I started," she said, "I went to the oldest person on the reservation and took notes and made sketches. I have notebooks full of information, but if I felt I didn't have enough, I looked in the history books. There are very few pictures of women in history books. I know because I looked and looked and looked. If I didn't find a woman's full picture, I might have found a picture of her head, but I couldn't see the skirts.

"The most fascinating thing, however, is the moccasins. It's amazing the different ways a pair of moccasins can be cut and look alike. One of the things I wonder about is how the first person who made a moccasin came to that conclusion. How did she ever figure it out and make it by tanning buckskin? That's something way above me."

Another part of traditional Apache culture that is passing away greatly concerns Mildred Cleghorn: the Apache language. She spoke only Apache when she was little because her mother and father spoke it at home. And because the words aren't heard in her part of the country anymore, "I know in my mind what I want to say. But when I say it, it doesn't come out that way. I've forgotten the use of the tongue and how to catch the word in my throat. Even on tape, when I hear it, one almost has to know, or remember, a little bit about the word to get the distinction."

Other traditions are not as endangered. In the summer of 1989 the tribe held a two-day cultural program at its complex grounds during which finger weaving, pottery, basketry, and beadwork were demonstrated. Children ages six to fourteen participated. But Mildred Cleghorn believes they still need much more instruction . . . and recognition.

"There are a few people here who feel that we wanted everyone to know there are still Chiricahua Apaches in Oklahoma," Mildred Cleghorn said firmly. "We stay very much to ourselves and we're quite independent of each other, even though we're all related. There is no reservation here, so we live differently than our cousins in Mescalero.

"We want a place where our people can learn and find out about one another. Our genealogy, for example. We need to gather the historical books about our people. For myself, I know nothing about the area of the country where my people came from. I've always wanted to know what it looked like and the conditions of it. For instance, folks talk about the Indian foods that the people had. They were all cactus foods and desert foods. Well, here in Oklahoma there's none of that around. Most of us get to taste our own food only when we visit in New Mexico. At least, we want to learn so we can know more about our history and our culture.

"We don't live a reservation life here," she said. "We live with our neighbors. My mother and father and some older folks used to say, 'Look around you, Mildred. There's not an Indian that lives around you. You have nothing but white people. You have to go to school.' That's all I ever heard: 'You have to go to school. You've got to learn the white man's way and you've got to do a little bit more if you can. Because you have to fight all the time for whatever you get, whatever you want.'

"I'm still fighting because we have a good way. I mean, the quality of life that the old folks lived was beautiful. It was loving and sharing, and what else can you ask? That's not the white man's way.

"Most of our Indian people are the same. Loving and sharing is the thing. We have extended family clear down to the umpteenth or seventeenth cousin, you might say. You're still my relative, you still have the same blood I have. It might be a drop, but it's there."

This sweeping, greathearted point of view is likely one of the reasons Mildred Cleghorn was selected by her peers as 1989 Indian of the Year. How does that choice make her feel? "Humble," she says simply. And then she repeats herself very softly. "Humble. I never thought I would be so honored."

But even as she expresses her feelings, her pride and her passion, in the language of her captors, one knows there is more, much more to be said. Not now, though. However, there is one last comment, one wish she makes for the Apache people in the future, ". . . to be Apaches throughout eternity." In so saying, Mildred Cleghorn speaks from the heart—for herself as well.

Ruey Haozous Darrow

Everything is going my way and has been for several years.

Ruey Darrow, the daughter of Apache prisoners of war Sam and Blossom Haozous, was going to be late for our appointment and cared enough about the inconvenience to call my hotel room several times to explain the reasons why. The weeklong meeting in Phoenix of Indian Health Service laboratory consultants from the western United States had two or three items on its late Friday afternoon agenda still needing attention, and it would be one hour, then another hour, then a half hour more before she could get away. I worried aloud about her being tired and suggested perhaps it would be better to meet the next day. Ruey Darrow wouldn't hear of it.

As I waited, I recalled our first meeting in Oklahoma at the Fort Sill Apache Tribe's celebration of the seventy-fifth year of their release from prison at Fort Sill. As one of only two white women in a room full of Mescalero and Fort Sill Apaches, I was definitely obvious but not uncomfortable. Looking out from behind a pot of boiled meat and chili, Mrs. Darrow saw me, put down the ladle, and came around a long table to introduce herself and personally welcome me to the event. Her actions were sophisticated, as was her ability to make me feel at home immediately. She took me by the arm and we walked in the direction of her family, all sitting and eating together, and, one by one, she introduced me: "This is my son Bill, this is my husband Bob, these are my daughters Debbie and Becky, my son Michael is around here someplace, and those are my grandchildren climbing around on that furniture."[38] I had met some of her family during the previous two days, but Mrs. Darrow had no way of knowing that: she had just arrived from Oklahoma City after conducting Indian Health Service business there. The Fort Sill Apache Tribe's anniversary coincided nicely with her whereabouts, and this lady was glad to be home. She doesn't get there often.

Ruey Darrow, a worldly-wise Apache woman, is extraordinary. She lives in Fort Cobb, Oklahoma, less than twenty miles from the Fort Sill Apache

Ruey Haozous Darrow.
(Photo by H. Henrietta Stockel)

Tribal Complex, but her office is nearly a thousand miles away in Aberdeen, South Dakota. Mrs. Darrow is a full-time professional Indian Health Service laboratory consultant who loves her job in the colder climate of the north country and enjoys the traveling she does during the course of her work. At sixty-three years of age, many other women would be thinking of retirement. Not Ruey Darrow. She holds no thought of slowing down or stopping. As a matter of fact, she has plans and ambitions for yet another career in the future, and I wanted her to tell me about them as soon as she could.

When the Indian Health Service's meeting was finally adjourned, Ruey Darrow softly knocked on the hotel door and then rushed into the room. Dropping on the end of a bed to catch her breath, she asked if she could include another woman in the evening's plans. It seems everyone else from Indian Health Service had gone to Flagstaff, 150 miles away, for dinner, and she didn't want her colleague to be alone in a strange town. I nodded in understanding, and we all drove off to look for a restaurant of her choice in a remote area north of Phoenix/Scottsdale. Ruey Darrow led the search for food that ended more than an hour later high atop a mountain. It was pitch black, the road was being repaired, we were running out of gas, and hunger was making us anxious when we finally found the restaurant and everyone relaxed. We ate a sumptuous cowboy meal served on tin plates in an Old West setting, and then we headed back down the mountain to the hotel, sixty miles away, for a quick sleep. The hour was very late.

Bright and early the next morning Mrs. Darrow was eager to begin the day. It was Saturday and she had free time to spend until Sunday at 7:00 A.M. when she was scheduled to fly back to Aberdeen. Along with an enthusiastic outlook on life that supplies her with nearly boundless energy, some of Mrs. Darrow's other characteristics were emerging. She is a woman who knows herself quite thoroughly and is therefore self-confident. She is well traveled and mentioned her trip to China in more than one conversation. It is probable that Ruey Darrow is equally comfortable consulting with eighteen or more medical laboratories for the Indian Health Service or on an airplane, in her living room, serving a pot of meat and chili at the tribal complex, or dancing with the *Gah'e*. Of these attributes, and others, that I glimpsed quite early in our time together, it was Ruey Darrow's bone-deep serenity that I noticed first.

"The Chiricahua were a peaceful people," wrote Michael Darrow.[39] No doubt that statement might be heatedly disputed, and with good reason, by those who hold the opposite point of view, but for those who share the belief, Ruey Darrow exemplifies Chiricahua peacefulness. And power. "I'd say my mother is a powerful woman," commented her son Michael.[40] It is her tranquility and sense of self that communicate power, not any impression of might or assertiveness, for Ruey Darrow is a petite, somewhat fragile-looking Apache woman. Despite a residual affliction from infantile paralysis in her left leg, she moves quickly and deliberately. For instance, in a Phoenix shopping center's huge parking lot, Mrs. Darrow was out of the car and almost at the front door of the store by the time the driver's door was closed and locked. Gone. In a flash. But, with a broad grin, she turned around to scan the parking lot for her companions.

Speaking in well-modulated tones, Mrs. Darrow doesn't hurry her answers. In conversation, one quickly learns to listen carefully to her words because it becomes obvious that she has considered each one before speaking. In response to a question about why she selected a career as a medical professional, she hesitated and then described a deeply personal situation.

"I was around medicine a lot as a result of having had polio and having all the subsequent corrective surgeries. I was particularly impressed with the surgeon, Dr. Donahue, who did the surgery. He was not only kind, he was very, very good. He has since become nationally known as an athletic/orthopedic doctor. Dr. Donahue was probably responsible for my interest."[41]

But that wasn't the full story, and so, a few minutes later, Mrs. Darrow returned to the topic, volunteering to discuss it more fully. "Originally I planned to be a physician," she said. "But after I started school and met Bob [her husband, Robert Darrow, a retired petroleum engineer], I decided that being a physician would not be the thing to do. Besides, at that time, everybody kept saying that I had to have a lot of money to do that. I didn't know then that I probably could have done it anyway, that lack of money wasn't as big a deterrent as it seemed." Any regrets? "Well, I was disappointed for many, many years," admitted Ruey Darrow. "Just recently I decided that that portion of my life is over. The time that I would have been a physician is over."

Having come to terms with a major disappointment, Ruey Darrow adds, "I would like to have my next profession be something different than healing." And then another one of this Apache woman's traits appears: honesty. "Right now," she said, "my job as a laboratory consultant is a means to get someplace else. The Indian Health Service is giving me a place and a time and a way to get what I'd like, and I'm taking full advantage of it. Indian Health Service would probably not appreciate knowing they are a means to an end, but I feel like they're getting the best I have to give." This is a woman definitely not afraid of honesty.

Sitting on large, soft cushions at the Heard Museum later in the morning, Mrs. Darrow watched an audiovisual presentation about Native Americans entitled *Our Voices, Our Land*. Moody Navajo flute music played in the background as Native Americans from many tribes expressed their concerns on film about environmental problems, the changing cultures, and vanishing traditional arts and crafts processes. In still photos on the three split screens, Indian elders with leather-wrinkled faces contrasted with children's smooth skin, old crackly voices worried about the parched earth, and young mothers and children smiled shyly at the camera. All the while the sad flute music wafted and drifted and filled in the silences. The audience of non-Indians was enraptured. Their faces were aglow and their bodies softened as the tones of the flute wove magic. Suddenly Mrs. Darrow, the only Indian in the small, intimate theater, leaned over and whispered, "Sounds like stress reduction music to me." Humor too— not irreverence—and a totally individualistic response from a seemingly thoroughly modern Apache woman.

Standing near one of Allan Houser's works of art in the courtyard of the Heard Museum that afternoon, she posed for photos behind the much-admired sculpture of a bronze goat girl herding a flock. From time to time tourists stopped to admire the statue. Mrs. Darrow joined them. No one, naturally, had the slightest idea that the artist was her brother, and as she paused to appreciate each bronze figure placed on the museum's lawns, it was as an art devotee rather than a sister. In her comments and facial expressions, she was able to separate sibling emotions from open admiration. In time, however, objectivity vanished. "Allan is such a wonderful person," she said.[42]

On one of our later visits we discussed some of the accomplishments of the Fort Sill Apaches. "If I'm not mistaken, Mildred [Cleghorn] and Michael [Darrow] tell me that, per capita, our tribe makes more money than any other tribe in the United States. My brother makes several million a year, so that kind of ups the range. We probably also have more education per capita, but again, we don't have a lot of people in the Fort Sill Apache Tribe and that has made a difference."[43] With regard to the tribe's educational attainments, Mrs. Darrow herself is probably one of the individuals responsible for the measurably high level of achievement. She holds a master of science degree in her field of interest, microbiology.[44]

Education was an important matter in Ruey Haozous's household when she was a youngster. "To get an education was something Papa talked about constantly," she said. "He told us specifically that if we wanted to get along and we wanted to have nice money, nice cars, and nice homes, we were going to have to make a living the way white people do. My mother agreed with him. She didn't want any of us to marry very young, and I don't think anybody did. I mean, we children were all twenty, maybe twenty-one years old, before we got married."

Ruey Haozous met Bob Darrow at the University of Oklahoma, and they have been together since. There are five grown children from their marriage: Robert, William, Michael, Becky, and Debbie. Grandchildren are present as well, and they are entering a world very much different from the one Ruey Haozous knew as a youngster.

The Haozous children attended elementary school near their parents' farm on the outskirts of Apache, Oklahoma, and then public high school in town. She remembered that the attitude of the community toward the Sam Haozous family was "different than it was toward other Indians. I'm not sure whether it was because my mother was half white or whether it was because we spoke English well or because we worked for good grades. All of us made fairly good grades in school, except for the two oldest children, who maybe didn't do as well because the circumstances were different when they were young. And we didn't associate with any other families except our own Apaches. That was only on weekends. The Kiowas and Comanches and Kiowa-Apaches lived around us and we went to school with them. They were still very, very Indian in their ways. As far as we were concerned, they did a lot of things that were considered immoral, and they were dirty. They had scabies and lice. There were a few, but not many, who were clean and neat, so we really didn't associate with them."[45]

Some might consider this arrogance, but Blossom and Sam Haozous were very perceptive parents who correctly envisioned a future for their children in which education, as a prerequisite for success, was a necessity. Very little was permitted to stand in the way of grooming their children to achieve status in the white man's world, and that included associating with individuals and groups who might sway the youngsters from the family's goals.

Early in her college career, Ruey Darrow had a bittersweet experience that she recalled with mixed emotions. "We ate mainly meat and potatoes at home," she said, "and I wasn't too familiar with salads. As a young woman on her own for the first time, I attended a buffet at the home of a young man I was seeing. I had no idea what to do with the salad dressing, so I put it on my potatoes. The boy I was with said it was all right, but the other people in the room were astonished."[46] In telling other stories about her youth, one of Ruey Darrow's favorite recollections is of her father as the family's storyteller. She said, "I used to love the coyote stories he told, but others that impressed me were when he talked about his mother. We used to think his mother was mean, but now I think she was more protective than anything else. My grandfather was a sharpshooter who would stay behind the Apaches as they fled. His job was to shoot at the enemy to give the group as much time as possible to get away. My grandfather was killed doing his job, and my grandmother was left with my father as a baby. He nursed at her breast until he was five years old because that was during the times when they didn't have anything to eat. He said he was a real big boy and remembered going out to play with bows and arrows, and then he'd come back and nurse. Evidently, it was a very difficult time.

"Papa also said that once he fell out of a tree. He broke his arm but was afraid to go back and tell his mother because she would get mad that he had hurt himself. He had been careless enough to get hurt and shouldn't have done that. Anyway, he finally went home and I can't remember now whether he said she whipped him or not, but it seems to me like she did."

It is easy to understand why a young girl would consider her grandmother's behavior "mean" when she heard this story, especially when it was told by her beloved father in the comfort and safety of their home. But the child Sam Haozous and his mother feared for their lives, and the Apache woman, with singlemindedness, was teaching her boy to be careful. After all, under those conditions of siege, anyone's carelessness might have resulted in the loss of many lives.

This matter-of-fact side of the Apache heritage is a legacy to subsequent generations of women, and it appears in Mrs. Darrow's philosophy about being separated from her own family. "I'm getting along very well without the family," she commented, "because everything is going my way and has been for several years. If you stop to think, you wonder whether you can keep it up forever. I'm not sure whether it's me that's causing all the good things to happen or not. But I think probably so.

"I worry a lot about Bob, but I can't live for him. His attitudes are kind of carved in stone and it's difficult for him to understand me or what I'm doing. When I talk to him I find there's a little wave here and there of 'what can I do so that you'll come home?' And it really doesn't have anything to do with him at all, which is unfortunate. Perhaps.

"For the most part, I don't ever let it become an issue with me because if I do, I can't give my full attention to what I'm doing now. Mainly, if I want to change it, I'm the one who's going to change it. And I don't want to change it. So, if I'm not willing to go ahead and make the changes, then I really can't expect anything else. It just goes on. . . .

"It has taken so many years and I don't really have any regrets about anything that I've ever done. I certainly am a product of what I was taught and the kind of life I've led, and now I am, for the first time, being me. Instead of Bob's wife, Debbie's mother, or Grandmother, it's my own identity for a change. I like it."

Lest anyone conclude that Ruey Darrow's attitudes are also "carved in stone," she talks about what it would really take to get her back home. "Actually, my family *is* important and should something happen to them or to Mildred [Cleghorn] or Kathleen [Kanseah], I would certainly leave the job. It would not be a matter of whether to or not. I would just do it because that's what I feel I should do. That's part of the way I was brought up."

Added to the influences she had at home were many experiences Mrs. Darrow had in working her way toward the advanced educational degree she now holds. "I've felt discrimination," she said, "but it happened mostly when I was younger and on the school bus. I just didn't respond to it. That was our way in all things. We just didn't respond. I believe there were a few remarks made when I was in high school, but I was already developing a belief that those people who are educated are not going to discriminate.

"There was one thing, however," she remembered, "when I was a freshman in college, but I don't think it was because I was Indian. I think it was because I was a woman. That year I was the university's Indian Princess. I think that year I was also one of the beauty queens for homecoming. It brought attention to me and that was kind of tough. A teacher flunked me in the second semester's composition course. The first time I made an A, but then he gave me an F. I finally went and complained about it. He must have had some difficulty with the university because he went on a long sabbatical at the end of that year. They gave one final test for everyone in all his classes and I got a good mark on that."

How would Mrs. Darrow grade Apache women today insofar as their being responsible for transmitting the Apache heritage to the current generation? "I don't think we have done a very good job of it," she declared. "What I have given to my children has been just the way I am. It has not been anything special. I have not made a specific difference. My children feel like they're Indian and they know they are, but that has not come about from being specifically taught anything. That's just because that's who I am. And I wouldn't know how to be otherwise. An Apache woman's responsibility is to do whatever is necessary to reflect well on your people, your family. There is an obligation to help them, or find some way to help them if they would accept it. At this point it would be easier to help women of tribes other than our own."

Plans for Ruey Darrow's future include helping young Native American women and children from all tribes. "I find there is a prevalent attitude that leads them to feel they are not good enough to do something, and I think that with enough practice, I can help even a few to think about themselves in another way. Perhaps they can then teach their children and, in turn, themselves adjust, not necessarily to the white man's or Indians' way, but just so they can be a little happier. The thing that's wrong is that so many of them are angry and unhappy, and it's so obvious. I run into it constantly. And it's easy to be angry and unhappy if you lie to yourself. I think we have to adjust our attitudes to be happy in spite of everything.

"I've been associating with women, and women are very strong. Men are still floating around—where will I go and what will I do, that sort of thing. But it's not necessarily all Indians doing that. A lot of men are like that regardless of whether they're white or Indian. Anyway, I wouldn't make an assumption like this if I'd only lived thirty or forty years. But at my age . . ."

Chronologically, Mrs. Darrow is approaching "elder" status, but in most ways she is in her prime. From this dual perspective, her views encompass many aspects of life and living. "Michael and I make cookies at Christmas," she said, "and we take them to the different Apache families in the area so they know they're not forgotten, that we remember them. And when we have my grandchildren with us, we take them along so they will know that's what we do. They don't really have any understanding of how I feel, but they need to know what we do."

And insofar as puberty ceremonies are concerned, they're fine with Ruey Darrow. "If the girl believes it's going to mean something to her, then I believe in it . . . for her. I think she can go in and out of that world and be the better for it. There are a lot of things that Apaches teach their girls in those ceremonies. It's eight days of concentrated teaching. Some of the women my age who had the ceremonies have profited, I think, not only because they learned something of how to present themselves to the world, but also it's just a way of life. A girl needs some help getting through the ceremony, even though she's been prepared from the time she was born. I don't know how the girls are doing as far as learning the Apache language is concerned. Kathleen says her girls understand some of it because she really talks a lot to them in the old language. But other folks have not done the same. It's kind of like you have to get far enough away from the puberty ceremony to be able to go back. And then you've developed a greater appreciation for it. Some of these people have not gone far enough away."

Ruey Darrow was referring not to physical distance but to emotional distance. One of the factors influencing the emotional distance from their heritage, and especially the sacred ceremonies, that the Apaches must endure is cultural assimilation in the American melting pot that trades ethnic identity for anonymity. Speaking as an Apache woman about mainstream society, she says, "In the other world, you aren't anything except just yourself. You're not any kind of tribe, you're not even a woman, you know. There, I'm just a laboratory consultant. That's my identity when I'm working. It doesn't occur to me that I look different or that I am different from anybody else. Actually, it's a kind of strain to be in the other world all the time.

"But most of the time it doesn't bother me, which is one of the reasons why I don't mind being by myself, away from my family. It gives me an opportunity to rejuvenate and then I can go back out and do whatever I need to do or whatever I want to do without difficulty.

"I do think Apache women have a place in the world, but not as 'Apache women.' Apache women have a place all right, and that's back with Apaches. Right now, defining myself is difficult because I feel like I'm a laboratory consultant most of the time. But then, a lot of times I feel more like a mother. 'Mother' always comes to mind. As far as being a woman is concerned, that is a distinction so ingrained that it doesn't mean much as far as an identity. Then again, when I'm with Indians, I realize that I'm an Indian. I mean, with Indians, you realize that you're a woman because there's a definite place for women.

"But I'm never just an Indian. I'm an Apache and I'm a woman. I'm an Apache woman. That's who I am. That's what I am. I've said that so many times, but then that's how I deeply feel. I'm an Apache woman."

Ceremonies
and
Celebrations

The ceremonies and celebrations described in this chapter occurred during the summer and autumn of 1989 on the grounds of the Mescalero Apache Reservation and the Fort Sill Apache Tribal Complex. Visitors are always encouraged to participate in these public events, which are publicized in local newspapers and advertised by colorful posters. The Apaches want to share their culture, and their hospitality is legendary.

MESCALERO APACHE PUBERTY CEREMONY
JULY 1989

Lulled by mile after mile of tall green pine trees, and then rounding a curve of the superhighway that bisects the Mescalero Apache

Reservation, a traveler suddenly sees tepees, tents, and clouds of brown dust rising from a nearby hillside. During the eighteen miles that have passed since the visitor left town, there has been practically no sign that Apaches live on this reservation. Only horses, wallowing belly deep in grasses that grow beside the road, have watched car after car speed by. Now, here it is: bona fide evidence that there are Indians around.

Gleaming in the sun and peeled clean of bark, very tall pine lodgepoles poke out from white canvas covers wrapped around dozens of tepees. And, near the tepees, tents for four people, some with squares of open netting to let the air in, some with flaps turned back for the same purpose, stand squarely at attention. Less visible from the highway are the bright blue and brown tarps covering another type of shelter—an approximately eight foot high by eight foot wide brush arbor made of branches of pine and other leafy trees held together and upright by wires, rawhide, rope, and natural forks in the wood. All these types of housing represent the ingenious, quite efficient, cool, and comfortable lodgings that the Apaches have been erecting for hundreds of years. Other brush arbors require even more intricate weaving of branches and boughs to form the walls and ceiling of long, large rooms for utilitarian functions such as cooking and frying to feed the hundreds of people who attend the Mescalero Apache Puberty Ceremony.

The closest exit farther along the well-maintained federal expressway bends a driver back toward the settlement and then up a steep incline to a dry, timeworn road. From the top, the view of the heavily wooded mountain range that distinguishes this reservation is spectacular, but the dirt road leads away from the vista and toward the ceremonial grounds.

On this day before the start of the annual event, pickup truck after pickup truck is in line to deposit its treasures of felled pine, poplar, and aspen trees, branches, and leaves on or near the sacred Apache grounds. This material, freshly cut in the surrounding forest, is used by the Apache fire crew to construct the natural brushy enclosures that will serve, for four days and nights, as kitchens, living quarters, and surcease from the hot sun for the families of the maidens who will be honored, tribal members, and guests.

The dust is choking. Each time the truck drivers rev their engines and spin their wheels as they come and go, shouting to each other, another cloud of fine brown sand floats over the tops of the other vehicles and inside open windows. It hasn't rained enough recently to pack the dust or even keep it close to the ground.

"Go ahead, go ahead," yelled an Apache hanging out of the passenger window of a truck coming directly at me, as he gestured toward the road back down off the hillside. "Get going!" He wiped the sweat and dirt from his face onto his forearm as his companion, the driver, waited to see what I would do. I called back and pointed behind him. "Can I get in there?" The fellow looked exasperated. "No! Not until tomorrow!" I turned right and started my descent off the hillside, slowly and carefully, unsure of myself, tailgated by the truck that undoubtedly was returning to the forest for another load of brush. In the rearview mirror I saw the men laughing.

The fire danger is extremely high, and it is also unusually warm, about ninety degrees as compared with the normal eighty-two or eighty-three at this time of year in Mescalero. Gray-black clouds roll over the tops of the ponderosa pine trees but don't stop. Even though there is a commanding need for moisture, I secretly hope in my heart that the showers will stay away until after the puberty ceremony. The maidens and their families have waited for this moment for as long as they can remember, and other people have traveled far to attend the ritual. It would be a shame if the weather didn't cooperate. But then again, maybe I have nothing to worry about as I see recreational vehicles, trucks with camper shells, trucks pulling horse trailers, and private cars of all makes and shapes heading for the area to find a good spot to park. It is important to be under or close to shade, especially if one's horses are expected to perform in the Apache rodeo that is also held during these four days. "This rodeo is not like anything you've ever seen," said one old-timer to a younger man in a conversation I overheard during a previous visit to Mescalero. "When the horn blows at the end of eight or ten seconds, these Apaches don't get off. They just hang on until they get thrown off or the animal quits. Apaches don't quit."

As I headed back toward town, I saw the rodeo bleachers on the left; the covered seats looked as if they would offer some shade on a hot, sunny day. An even more interesting sight, though, was a young Apache girl, perhaps no more than three years old, leading a tall, sturdy, fat stallion, his cocoa brown coat glistening with sweat, across a field. She was only a little taller than the horse's knees, but what she lacked in height she made up in self-confidence as she marched toward her family's camper and then deftly tethered the horse to a tree where he would, much later, spend a cool night among the tall pines.

At sunrise the next morning, the ceremonies began with the men of the tribe building a medicine tepee, a sacred structure opening to the east. Unlike their counterparts, however, the lodgepoles supporting the medicine tepee were not peeled. The bark remained intact, as did the leafy branches at the top of the twenty-five or thirty-foot-tall young trees. Each thin pole served a clear purpose, either as a supporting part of the framework or as a ceremonial/symbolic segment of the whole. A canvas cloth wrapped the lodgepoles only at the top but allowed branches to wave freely in the hot breezes that blew across the ceremonial grounds, even at seven o'clock in the morning. Closer to the ground, Apache men piled varieties of brush up and down the lodgepoles, curling pliable smaller boughs around larger branches, creating vertical thickets that rose and descended along the entire height of the framework. Limbs, twigs, tendrils, all things green and leafy, went into the construction of the tepee that would enclose the maidens during the ceremony.

At the same time, Apache women were busy in the long brush arbors. Far from the medicine tepee, under the shade of layers of green, at least six middle-aged women were slapping kneaded dough between their hands, making certain it was rounded exactly and was at least the size of a tortilla. Then they passed it to other women who stood ready, in front of black, bubbling cauldrons of hot lard, to drop the bread dough into the fat. With long, forked sticks these women swished the batter around until it became browned and harder. Then it was flipped over, stirred around again for a shorter time, and lifted out of the boiling lard with the stick. Visitors and tribal members walked in and out of the brush arbor, all with outstretched hands covered with paper towels, waiting for the hot Apache fry bread to fall with a plop into their lives. The paper towels were formed into a cuff to hold the fry bread as a hungry breakfaster bit into it with great delight. Other tribes may add powdered sugar, cinnamon, or honey to their fry bread, but the Apaches eat it as is. No frills disguise the unique flavor of this tasty dish.

Elbys Hugar was among the women volunteering to shape the raw dough when I saw her on the morning of July 1, 1989, but before she took her turn cooking, she walked with me across the ceremonial grounds to the long, narrow brush arbor where two fires were burning. "These will never go out during the four days," she said.[1] "The people use these fires for many things during the days of the ceremony." Despite the coolness afforded by the brush, it was becoming quite hot near the fires, so we walked on toward the cooking arbor. Mrs. Hugar tore a paper towel off one of many rolls laying on wooden tables and stood behind a woman who was stirring fry bread in the fat. "Here," she said as she held out her paper towel–covered hand. "Put it here." She tapped the woman's shoulder. The fry bread coming out of the lard on a stick looked made to order for a hungry visitor. "The families of the girls supply the food for the four days," Mrs. Hugar explained. "All the food is free. There will be boiled meat, beans, fry bread, mesquite pudding, and coffee or Kool-Aid for the people. Three times a day. It's all cooked here on the feast grounds and will be served after the puberty ceremony."

At almost 8:00 A.M. four young girls dressed in exquisitely beaded buckskin dresses and beaded moccasins, accompanied by godmothers, godfathers, and sponsors, crossed the ceremonial grounds and walked, heads bowed and hands folded in front of them, toward the medicine tepee. There they knelt on a floor of deep green cattail stalks that had been especially gathered for the occasion. The girls faced east and received the blessing of the medicine men and others, beginning the ceremony. No one was permitted to walk across the sacred grounds until the ritual was concluded, but Apaches lined up in a long row on either side of the medicine tepee, forming a passageway for the girls to run through. One Apache man kept the corridor to a certain width by walking along the inside area and urging everyone to stand back.

Activities in the medicine tepee continued but were occasionally obscured from public view by the medicine men and others performing sacred actions. There were many individuals inside the medicine tepee, but when the time for a certain part of the ritual arrived, everyone moved aside. Older women laid pieces of buckskin on the ground, and the girls fell facedown upon the soft skins. The sponsors massaged the maidens and then helped them back up on their feet. The next part of the ceremony required the girls to run toward the east and around a basket four times. When this was concluded, Apache woven baskets full of candy and other treasures, symbolizing abundance, were dumped over the maidens' heads. Simultaneously, four pickup trucks, one from each of the girls' families, arrived on the grounds with their beds full of candy and fruit. Apaches stood in the beds of the trucks and threw their contents to a crowd of people, all of whom knew what was coming and scurried to catch the food in midair or pick it up off the ground. That portion of the puberty ceremony was then concluded.

After a short delay, family members brought food to the center of the ceremonial grounds from the brush arbors. Boiled meat was served in large pots placed directly on the ground. There were beans, chili, fry bread, mesquite pudding, and galvanized buckets full of coffee and Kool-Aid. Paper cups, bowls, and plates were provided. The supply of food was rapidly eaten and more was brought out and served until, suddenly, the meal was over. People milled around, talking with one another, waving at each other, and driving off in their cars and trucks, to return later for the next group of activities. The maidens had retired to their individual tepees with their families and attendants.

At the bottom of the hill, just below the ceremonial grounds, vehicles full of Apaches and non-Indians were finding shady spaces to park. Coolers were lifted out of truckbeds or pulled out of automobiles and placed on the ground under trees, behind bushes, or in the shadow of horses tethered to nearby posts. Blankets, tablecloths, bedspreads, and other covers were held to the earth with stones or coolers or children's toys. People donned sun hats, sombreros, cowboy hats, and ducks' bills advertising everything from nails to rodeos, from moving vans to political parties. A few brave individuals set up portable folding chairs along the roadway out in the blazing sun to be assured of a prime spot. The parade, with this year's theme of "Honoring Bearers of Tradition," would be coming soon.

Near the tribal administration offices, the post office, and the cultural center, floats were lining up and the paraders were milling around, talking and laughing and admiring each other's costumes. Horses snorted unhappily and pawed the asphalt parking lot, eager to start. No one was clearly in charge, yet all was orderly and organized. Police cars slowly cruised the area, their occupants perhaps not so much interested in wrong-doers in the vicinity on this puberty ceremony weekend as in where the head of the line was so they could get into position. The law enforcement vehicles were scheduled to lead the parade.

And so they did, not too much later, their sirens blaring and lights flashing, led by a policeman on a motorcycle. Side by side the first two cars, accompanied by the same motorcyclist who had been driving among the vehicles and encircling the first two or three rows of the police cars in the procession, climbed the slight rise from the center of the village, crossed the federal highway, and moved on toward the ceremonial grounds. People stepped into their path to take a photo, to wave, or just to stare.

Sheriffs' posses from surrounding towns sent their best-looking delegations, all riding proudly astride magnificent horseflesh, glistening from sweat in the late morning sun. The parade marshall, Ceda Magoosh-Shanta, a female descendant of both the Chiricahua and the Lipan Apache bands, sat in the middle of a float surrounded by greenery from the forest and members of her family, smiling and turning from right to left as she slowly passed the onlookers.

Wearing an Apache beadwork tiara and a traditional Apache dress, Miss Mescalero of 1989, a young lady by the name of Pamela Kaydoso (Elbys Hugar's granddaughter), rode in a long white limousine, the top part of her body emerging through an opening in the vehicle's roof. As she passed her family's home along the parade route, an excited look crossed her face and she waved them her pleasure.

Flags flying high above her, the Ruidoso (N.M.) High School Indian Club Princess sat on her own float with a male companion as dozens of children on horseback wearing buckskin or velveteen (if they were Navajo) or dressed as warriors led, followed, or rode between the colorful entries. Bingo of Mescalero sponsored a float with a tepee and a brush arbor on it. As this conveyance moved along, it passed directly beside the hill on which the real tepees and brush arbors sat.

Two huge trucks carrying enormous logs from the forest and planks cut from those logs chugged and hauled and coughed their way up the hill to demonstrate one of the tribe's successful industries. A Navajo band dressed in white-and-turquoise satin marched and played their instruments as the spectators applauded. And then, too soon, it seemed finished; but at the end of the long line of marchers and parade vehicles was a striking sight: a warrior and his maiden sitting straight as yucca stalks atop their horses. His entire face painted a ghostly yellow, this young man with classic Apache features held his long, long black hair, falling over his ears and shoulders, in place with a red headband. He rode without a saddle, sitting just on some red-and-gray blankets thrown over his steed's back, and carried a yellow lance in his left hand. He wore a royal blue Indian shirt, shiny, as if it were made of silk, and denim trousers. In his right hand he held the reins of his maiden's horse while she, dressed in a traditional cotton Apache dress of pale lavender and high white doeskin moccasins, also rode atop blankets and without a saddle beside him. These two parade participants, like all the other entries, passed too quickly toward an area near the rodeo grounds where they dismounted and resumed their usual festive activities. The parade was over.

Crowds lining the frontage road packed up their belongings, old folks, and children, and scattered. Some returned to the ceremonial grounds and waited for the noon meal to be served, others went to their homes or the homes of relatives or back to their temporary camp. Visitors searched for shelter from the unusually hot summer sun. The afternoon activities were scheduled to begin at around one o'clock with two simultaneous events— a rodeo and a contest dancing.

The rodeo began on time, but contest dancing was postponed because of the heat, and then eventually canceled. Music provided by the Navajo Nation band filled the air as old friends met and greeted each other, or simply sat in the shade of a brush arbor and watched the passersby. The maidens stayed in their tepees and rested. Everyone was waiting for nightfall when the *Gah'e* would appear at the ceremonial grounds. Wooden logs had been split and were stacked to the side of the dance arena in a pile the shape of a tepee in anticipation of the event, when they would be sacrificed in a bonfire, blazing in the center of the ceremonial grounds not far from the medicine tepee and bright enough to turn the mountain night blackness into glowing orange. Around this ancient symbol the Mountain Spirit dancers would dance.

As the hour grew late, people found seats in the bleachers surrounding the ceremonial grounds on two sides. A disembodied voice, basso profundo in timbre, announced the time over the loudspeaker system about every fifteen minutes. As 8:30 P.M. arrived, night began to descend quickly in the Mescalero Apache forest. Two Apache fire starters walked to the center of the ceremonial grounds, knelt on the earth, hunched over their tools, and began to create fire. Wisps of smoke rose from their work and then were blown away by the breeze. As it grew cooler, spectators donned jackets, wrapped themselves in blankets or rugs, or just pretended they were still warm. Children were hugged closer and baby shoes put on tiny feet. The fire starters labored diligently, but the light winds were stubborn. Upon a signal from the men, a hot log was brought to the center of the arena from inside a brush arbor used for cooking. The fire was started, and other logs from the side pile were delivered and thrown onto the now-blazing stack. Several onlookers applauded, but the sound was lost among the rustling in the bleachers.

The announcer explained that the *Gah'e* were preparing themselves for this sacred aspect of the ceremonial by praying and receiving blessings. He reminded the audience that, although festive, what they were about to witness was holy in the eyes of the Apache people. He went into no further detail or description, and soon afterward everyone heard the soft, steady tinkle of tiny bells approaching from the east toward the ceremonial grounds.

Out of the darkness they appeared—four men, their chests and arms painted black with white designs. Wearing fringed yellow buckskin skirts with jingles, and moccasins, they shuffled, single file, toward the fire. On their heads, covered with black cloths, were the magnificent headdresses used only by the *Gah'e* when they dance: wooden crowns with tall, painted spikes penetrating the night. In their hands they held short staffs painted with the symbols of a people long persecuted, yet vital, resilient, and rich in heritage. Pointing at the fire, they slowly danced toward it, followed by a clown who hopped, skipped, and acted as if he wasn't part of the group.

The *Gah'e* circled the blaze to their left and danced toward the medicine tepee, which they approached from the four directions, still in a line, still moving their feet in a symbolic step. It was when the dancers came around the back of the tepee that the sound they were making became discernible. Not a cry, not a moan, not an imitation of a bird's call, this unique and ancient tone was in four parts, each following the other immediately. To the uninitiated it might have sounded like an owl's hoot, but the notes were nearly soprano and were more of a call to or from the spirit world than an earthly harmonic. As they returned toward the fire, in unending rhythm, a few women wrapped in shawls began to dance on the grounds to the rear of the *Gah'e*. The clown continued to frolic and amuse onlookers. After the approach to the four directions around the fire had been completed, the *Gah'e* danced off to the east, to be replaced in a few minutes' time by another troop of *Gah'e*, painted somewhat differently but following the same dance patterns. A third group appeared after the second, this one with two clowns. "The littlest one is my nephew," said Elbys Hugar.[2]

At the conclusion of this portion of the puberty ceremony, all three troops of *Gah'e* danced together around the fire, all making the same spiritual sound, all followed by their clowns. The maidens appeared and went to the medicine tepee, where a fire hole had been dug in the ground and a fire begun. More puberty rites were conducted on into the cool night. Visitors began leaving, but at the entrance gate, even though the hour was late, many more were still arriving.

In the morning, one of the last logs to be placed on the pyre was still smoking. But, mysteriously, the ashes from those dozens of logs formed only a thin ground cover, and the soil around the area of the fire was undisturbed, free of footprints. It was as if the *Gah'e* had never been there.

MESCALERO APACHE HERITAGE DAY,
AUGUST 1989

An Apache woman, arms and fingers heavy with turquoise-and-silver jewelry, confidently approached the microphone, adjusted her position, planted her feet, leaned forward, and grasped both sides of the lectern with strong, capable hands. As she spoke clearly, her words bounced off the portable platform decorated with green boughs, floated through the thin mountain morning air, and then sank into thick green grass outside the cultural center. The audience, seated on folding chairs, listened respectfully and stared at the attractive woman dressed in white. Evelyn Breuninger, an elected member of the Mescalero Apache Tribal Council and chairman of the council's Community Services Subcommittee, had worked hard and long to produce the events of this day—the first Heritage Day in Mescalero Apache history—and on August 19 she was onstage with Chairman Wendell Chino to begin the celebration.

Evelyn Breuninger is a powerful woman who expresses her natural energy in several ways: in the charm she exudes, in the friendly smile that frequently fills her face, in her stylish wardrobe, and in her careful use of the English language with a charming Apache accent. With Elbys Hugar, she coauthored the *Mescalero Apache Dictionary* and thus recorded for all time this ancient, complicated language. But on Heritage Day Mrs. Breuninger wasn't focusing on her personal accomplishments. She was much more concerned with the smooth flow of the program. This Apache woman needn't have worried. As with most things Evelyn Breuninger does, this special celebration would be a big success.

Mescalero Apache Tribal Chairman Wendell Chino spoke early in the program. The chief's verbal and persuasive skills are legendary among those he meets with or addresses in public forums, but, to this listener who is familiar with his style, Mr. Chino exceeded himself on Heritage Day. He talked about the history and culture of the Apache people and described a legacy of strengths and traditions that has endured since days of old. The chairman rose high on his toes, jabbed the air with his fingers and his fist, and articulately portrayed a group of Americans hunted and hounded by a government determined to forcefully subdue any opposition to official policies. Yet the Apaches survived and preserved their ways, reminded Mr. Chino, which was no small feat when their society was under constant siege. He called the names of the warriors, the scouts, the leaders, and paid respect to the women who remained behind. He urged young people to remember their cultural inheritance and discounted the desirability of becoming part of the mainstream. He praised the members of the tribe who planned and implemented Heritage Day. Time and time again Mr. Chino roused the audience's emotions with his eloquence, his command of the English language, and his commitment to the Mescalero Apache people. Mr. Chino's oratory enthralled, excited, and literally held everyone's total attention until the very last word. Then he simply turned from the microphone and took his seat. For long seconds there was no sound and no movement in the audience. Everyone, regardless of cultural background, felt the power of his speech . . . and it was virtually immobilizing.

Children enrolled in the Mescalero Apache Headstart program picked up the beat as they performed the Apache war dance accompanied by adult singers and drummers. Costumed and with painted faces, about a dozen kids imitated warriors of old. One little girl wearing a yellow cotton dress and high brown moccasins carried a knife in a holster strapped around her waist. At the sound of certain vocalized musical notes, she pulled out the knife, bent over at the waist, and, with a toss of her long black hair, pointed the weapon at an unseen enemy. All the while the other children were dancing around her. When the rhythm of the songs and drumbeat changed, she replaced the knife in the leather holster and found a young boy with whom she could lock arms and dance socially. Back and forth they moved, side by side, sometimes together and sometimes apart, but always acutely aware of their feet. The audience was charmed; the elders were enchanted.

Sometime later Evelyn Breuninger called the names of the elders who would be introduced and honored. Mack Bigmouth, in his nineties, haltingly walked up to the platform, leaning on a cane. He turned and faced the audience and nodded his head in greeting before he slowly returned to his seat. Edna Comanche, perky and bright and in her eighties, was happy to talk privately with everyone about her years as a prisoner of war and her family history. Katherine Kenoi, holding an umbrella over her head to protect herself from the sun and oncoming rain, was less ebullient. She only responded shyly when she heard her name. Unable to attend because of health or other reasons, but still mentioned, were Nona Blake, Pasquala Cojo, and Annie Guydelkon.

As if in contrast to the elders, Miss Mescalero of 1989, Pamela Kaydoso, read a poem beseeching young people to remember their heritage, lest it be lost forever. Her voice wavered, her chin trembled, but she completed the poem before she stepped aside and relinquished the microphone to a former Miss Mescalero. This young woman acknowledged several others, all of whom have represented the tribe as Princesses. Many wore beaded tiaras and their beautiful buckskin puberty dresses.

Next, a group of women climbed on stage and sang a few of the traditional songs. Elbys Hugar, sitting in the shade outside the cultural center, took it as long as she could. All at once she rose and approached the stage. Lifting the skirt of her red camp dress up to her ankles, she walked up the steps of the platform and stood behind the singers. Mrs. Hugar, not a scheduled part of this performance, started to sing along. When the singers realized she had joined them, they took a half step aside to make room. Soon, Mrs. Hugar had worked her way forward and was close to the microphone. Her soft voice filled the open spaces. "I couldn't help it," she said later. "I just had to sing with them."[3] The reservation's Catholic priest strummed his guitar and sang songs of his own choosing when the women were finished. Then he retired to the church's booth and sold chances on a painting of Jesus.

Not too long after the music concluded, one of the Tribal Council members stood on the grass in front of the stage. With the help of a model dressed in her puberty dress, he described every symbol on the beaded garment and its meaning. Following that, a contest was held in which women modeled their own clothing creations. Nobody won because it started raining. Most everyone ran for shelter to the cultural center. Mrs. Hugar loved having the crowd in her quarters and welcomed all the dripping-wet folks as they hurried inside.

While the activities at the podium were being held, Apache life in the old days was demonstrated under a long row of brush arbors. Hides were soaked in water prior to being tanned, mescal was cooked in a pit beneath a layer of stones, and three grandmotherly Apache women were up to their elbows in fresh blood as they butchered an animal. Women described cradleboard making, fire starting, beadwork, and doll making. Mrs. Hugar conducted tours of the Cultural Center. Arts-and-crafts booths offered a variety of merchandise and baked goods.

And, typical of the Apache people's hospitality, a free lunch was served to all those in attendance, courtesy of the Mescalero Apache Tribe.

When asked months later if she planned to have another Heritage Day program next year, Evelyn Breuninger got a glazed look in her eyes. "I don't know," she said. "It's a lot of work."[4] Reminded of the occasion's rousing success and cultural worth, she smiled, "Yes, I have heard people liked it. Thank you for saying so."

FORT SILL APACHE TRIBE,
SEVENTY-FIFTH ANNIVERSARY OF FREEDOM,
SEPTEMBER 1989

Standing alone for just a moment in bright Oklahoma sunshine, Mildred Cleghorn shivered as she wrapped herself in a thick, robin's-egg-blue wool Pendleton blanket. Pulling the ankle-length wrap up to cover her ears and silver gray hair, she hunkered down into the folds. One would think it was December or January, or that the scene was set somewhere in the northern reaches of the country, Alaska maybe. No. This was Apache, Oklahoma, and the date was September 23, 1989. Unseasonable weather, the result of Hurricane Hugo slamming into the coastline one thousand miles to the east, brought cold winds blowing more than twenty-five miles per hour across the hills and valleys of the southern part of the landlocked state. Radio reports estimated the temperature, including the wind-chill factor, to be below freezing, threatening to interfere with the celebration of the Fort Sill Apache Tribe's seventy-fifth anniversary of freedom. Less hardy souls sought cover in their vehicles, but Mrs. Cleghorn strolled around the grounds of the tribal complex, greeted old friends and visitors, smiled pleasantly, and pretended she was warm. Every now and then she sniffled, brought a paper tissue out from under the Pendleton, and blew her nose. Only rarely was she absent from the center of activities, and then just for a short period of time as she briefly retreated into her car for a respite from the wind. This Apache woman had much to celebrate and, in true Apache fashion, permitted very little to interrupt her plans.

The festivities actually began two days earlier when the tribe sponsored a supper for everyone arriving to share in the celebration. Boiled meat, hash, potatoes, salad, desserts, soft drinks, and coffee were dished out in the kitchen of one of the buildings to the rear of the complex. The arrivals, most of them from the Mescalero Apache Reservation five hundred miles away, appeared regularly at the door and were happily welcomed. Greetings were shouted, especially when a Mescalero medicine man jerked open the screen door and then joked about its poor condition and torn screen. "Why don't you fix it instead of complaining?" Mrs. Cleghorn shot back with a broad grin. "It's good to see you anyway. C'mon in." The medicine man waved his cowboy hat, sat at a long banquet table, and waited to be served supper by his daughter-in-law. Afterward, the Fort Sill and Mescalero Apaches all went their separate ways, promising to return the next day, when scheduled activities would start.

Mildred Cleghorn fixed a plate piled high with food to take to her nephew, Leland Michael Darrow (most everyone calls him by his middle name), who had remained at his home beading a leather purse to be presented to Garnett Mithlo Tate, the last child born in captivity. As one of very few Fort Sill Apaches actively doing traditional craftwork, Mr. Darrow was also making moccasins for Allan Houser, the first child born in freedom. Mrs. Tate and Mr. Houser were the honored guests at the anniversary celebration, formally set for September 23.

Arriving at the Darrow house, seventeen miles away from the tribal complex, Mrs. Cleghorn rang her nephew's doorbell and presented him with the plate of food. Mr. Darrow graciously welcomed her to the living room and, with a flourish, presented her with a needle and thread. He pointed to the purse and loose beads on an end table under bright lamplight and retired to the kitchen to eat the food. Mrs. Cleghorn pulled up a hassock and continued Michael's work of beading the purse. After supper, Michael brought the soles of the moccasins into the living room. First, he laboriously punched holes with a needle in the sides of the tough cowhide so the soft tops of the moccasins could be attached. Before long, his fingers and hands were sore and red, but he continued, all the while supervising his Aunt Mildred from across the room and commenting on her skills. She didn't appreciate his remarks, but she shrugged them off and concentrated on picking up several beads with the tip of the needle and sewing them onto the leather.

Kathleen Kanseah, who accompanied Mrs. Cleghorn to the house, sat on the nappy rug and spread white paper over the coffee table. She unfurled a roll of leather that would form the tops of the moccasins. Taking an old toothbrush in her hand, she dipped it in yellow pigment that Blossom Haozous had saved in a round metal can resembling a small snuff or chewing tobacco container. Gently, Mrs. Kanseah brushed the yellow powder onto the outside portion of the hide with long strokes, making certain that the density of the color was the same across the skin. Every so often she held the hide up to the light, turned it over in her hands, and examined the entire piece as if it were a foreign object, something she had never seen before. When she was satisfied that her work would be acceptable to Michael's critical eye, she continued stroking the pigment onto the skin. Finally, the entire strip of leather had been colored a soft yellow, symbolic of the sacred Apache pollen, and it was ready for inspection. Peering closely under a strong light at every inch, Michael Darrow agreed it was nearly perfect and took the skin outside to slap it up against a tree trunk to remove the excess pigment. When he returned to the living room, Mrs. Kanseah had already started the other piece. It was treated exactly the same as the first, including slapping it against a tree in the dead of night. Patching the round holes in the leather was her last task, and it took even longer than pigmenting did. When she finished sewing small leather circles over the holes, they were colored, too, and then both skins were presented to Michael for attaching to the cowhide soles.

Meanwhile, Mrs. Cleghorn chatted merrily with friends and relatives in the room as she stitched glass beads onto the purse and created colored fringes out of multicolored beads. She good-naturedly teased Michael and Kathleen about how far along she was in her project as compared with their work, and they reminisced about previous occasions when they had been together, preparing for other festivities. She shared a secret about how she and Michael argue frequently when they design and create traditional crafts: often, he insists he is correct in his procedures and she insists she is correct in her ways, which are contrary to his. As proof, she refers to her age and cites the fact that she has learned from the elders, is an elder herself, etc., etc., etc. Michael usually remains unmoved and always stands his ground. Who wins? Nobody would say.

Very late that evening, the traditional Apache beadwork ceased at the Darrow house, still unfinished, and the guests departed. Michael continued attaching the tops of the moccasins to the soles. It was terribly difficult work, but something he said he enjoyed—especially because they were to be presented to Allan Houser, a member of the Fort Sill Apache Tribe and also Michael Darrow's uncle. Not incidentally, Michael was also planning to be busy the next day cooking meat with Santa Fe red chili for the festivities. His time was limited.

The next morning brought busy activities to the tribal complex offices. Pots of chili and beans were cooking, meat was boiling, watermelons were arriving, and the beadwork continued. In the afternoon, a special traditional arts-and-crafts demonstration was held during which several women from Mescalero participated.

One younger Apache woman described and discussed the use and origin of camp dresses, and the significance of the puberty dress, demonstrating handmade jingles, strips of uncut fringe, as well as the buckskin always used in making the dress. She described the Chiricahua moccasins, which are different from all other Apache boots because of the toe guard.

Another Apache woman from New Mexico described cradleboards with oak or yucca frames, bound by buckskin straps and backed with yucca stalks. These are split in half and laced with buckskin. The half-moon crown that covers a baby's head has four slits if the occupant is a boy. The buckskin lace tie-ins are placed on the right for a girl, on the left for a boy. The cradleboard itself is made four days or more after the birth of the baby.

A special exhibit of natural medicines, including grasses and other ingredients used in healing teas, was shown to an attentive audience by Mary Pena, the director of traditional programs on the Mescalero Apache Reservation. Mrs. Pena discussed herbs, roots, and plants used by the Apaches in the old days and demonstrated these on posters, which recorded descriptions of their uses and applications, as well as their Apache names.

Mildred Cleghorn helped hang this demonstration on the walls and lean the posters against the blackboard before she participated in another of Mrs. Pena's demonstrations—an old Apache game called slapstick.

This child's game uses sticks and stones placed in a circle and four sticks, each of which has several "moves" on it. A player drops the sticks, determines how many "moves" he can make around the circle, and if the number falls in predetermined spaces, he is "out." The player remaining after all the others are "out" is, of course, the winner. Mrs. Pena sat down on the floor and encouraged everyone to participate, regardless of age. Soon after hearing the children's squeals and shouts of glee, adults were also on the floor sharing in the fun.

That evening another feast was served by the Fort Sill Apache Tribe. A long folding table was set up near the kitchen, with food to be served directly from large pots. More than a hundred hungry Apaches were lined up in several rows waiting for supper. First, however, the Mescalero Apache medicine man blessed the food by praying over it in the language of his ancestors. Today's Apaches—men, women, and children—stood silently with bowed heads. No one coughed, no one shuffled their feet, the children didn't move, and some of the men held their cowboy hats in their hands. For a long, long time the medicine man prayed in tones that rose and fell as he scattered yellow pollen around the food. When he was finished, it was time to eat. Behind the large serving pots, Mildred Cleghorn, Ruey Darrow, and other Apache women lifted ladles and filled the plates. Others passed out the bread and styrofoam cups of soft drinks or hot coffee. The noise level at the long tables filling the room rose gradually, and then laughter rang out. Conversations from one side of the room to the other were common. Well-fed children started climbing on the day-care equipment and playing together.

Outside, a few hundred feet away, Apache men piled logs and kindling wood in the shape of a tepee in preparation for the *Gah'e*. By the time supper was finished, the fire was blazing and the Apache people were strolling to the area, carrying aluminum chairs, blankets, and heavy jackets. Making themselves comfortable, they settled in for a long night of dancing and socializing.

The official program began the next afternoon, despite the cold winds, when Apache, Comanche, and Kiowa men faced the east and danced the Gourd Dance. To the accompaniment of singers and drummers, women wrapped themselves in colorful shawls and danced in place as the men held gourds in their hands and rattled them and moved their feet in rhythm with the music. A little later an Apache woman sang the invocation and the welcome was given by Mrs. Cleghorn. Presentation of the completed beaded purse to Garnett Mithlo Tate and the moccasins to Allan Houser was made by one of the men of the Fort Sill Apache Tribe as Mrs. Cleghorn stood by and witnessed the events. Both honorees gave short speeches expressing their thanks. The food was catered on this special occasion, and once again the Apaches lined up with plates in their hands. A giveaway was held in which all sorts of foodstuffs were distributed, mainly to the children. The Fort Sill Apache Tribe sold caps, tee shirts, and sweatshirts to raise operating capital. A representative of the U.S. Census Bureau stood beside a table and took the names of those who chose to register for the 1990 census. The 1989 Fort Sill Apache Princess mingled in the crowd and shook hands while the singers and drummers went on for hours. As dusk was coming on, the men again piled logs and kindling in the center of the dance grounds and the crowd made themselves comfortable for the evening. The *Gah'e* would be dancing soon.

As the fire blazed that night, Mildred Cleghorn brought her chair to a place beside Kathleen Kanseah and Ruey Darrow. She slipped out of the blue blanket cocoon for a short while and stared into the fire. In front of her, three groups of *Gah'e* danced and prayed in honor of the seventy-fifth anniversary of the Fort Sill Apaches' release from imprisonment. Behind her, a crowd of nearly 250 participants shared in the celebration. All around her, the rhythmic intonations of drums and beloved Apache sacred songs filled the night. She took a deep breath, wrapped the blanket around her again, and led Kathleen and Ruey out onto the dance ground. These three Apache women, honoring their ancestors and their heritage, then stepped into the drumbeat and danced and prayed with the *Gah'e*, just as Apache women have always done.

Seated beside me on aluminum chairs in the soft blue-black velvet of an Oklahoma summer night were Mildred Cleghorn and Kathleen Kanseah. Elbys Hugar, nursing a sore throat and a dry, hacking cough, was with her family just a dozen or so yards to the north. One hundred or more people, mostly strangers to me, were milling around and placing their own aluminum chairs in a large circle surrounding the dance grounds at Indian City, USA. The many Native Americans present had been celebrating the dedication of the bronze bust of Cochise and Mrs. Cleghorn's designation as 1989 Indian of the Year. Now it was time for Apache women to don their shawls and pay tribute to their heritage in the ways Apache women have always done—by dancing with the *Gah'e*.

Elbys Hugar had told me previously that women are not permitted to dance with the *Gah'e* without wearing shawls over their shoulders. Shawlless for too long, I finally invested fifty dollars in a solid black wrap with green trim—a high price for me since my shoestring budget was getting tighter and tighter. I thought my shawl was beautiful, the nicest one for sale on the rack at the Indian City gift shop, but perhaps it was a bit too warm for the summer night air. Time would tell.

In preparation, Apache fire starters carefully stacked heavy logs in the shape of a tepee over cold silver ashes, leftovers from recent dances, in the center of the arena. Then they shoved kindling inside the structure that was so thick it might burn forever. Just that afternoon the editor of the local newspaper confided that she had no idea where the Apaches would find enough firewood in the flatlands of Anadarko, but when it comes to gathering what the ritual requires, Apaches are experts. Thrown onto a pile just a short distance from the dance grounds were all shapes of deadwood—twigs, branches, stumps, roots, you name it—destined to be part of the pyre.

As everyone looked forward to the sacred ceremony, Mrs. Cleghorn and Mrs. Kanseah greeted wellwishers who wandered by, stopped for conversation or a hug, and shared the events of their lives. The two women learned who got married, who gave birth, who was working where, and a lot more from their friends and acquaintances. In response to comments from a few visitors, Mrs. Cleghorn took a "weekly minder" notebook out of her purse and, by the glow of the now-blazing fire, noted changes of addresses, new telephone numbers, and rescheduled appointments. Children abounded; some belonged to the Cleghorn extended family, some to the Kanseah clan, some to the Naiche group across the way, and the rest to all the tribes present. Among others there were Comanches, Kiowas, Wichitas, Delawares, Sac and Fox, Otos, Cherokees, Choctaws, Chickasaws, Muscogees, and Seminoles. All were waiting for the *Gah'e.*

As she heard the unmistakable sounds of the oncoming *Gah'e*—dozens of jingles swishing on fringed, ankle-length buckskin skirts—Mrs. Cleghorn unzipped her nylon backpack and removed several shawls. In the orange firelight she distributed the smaller ones to the Kanseah grand-daughters before she and Mrs. Kanseah wrapped their shoulders in the larger garments.

Then the *Gah'e* slipped out of the night, four of them, followed by a white-painted, bare-chested boy wearing shorts. Skipping close behind the dancers, the youth had a cowbell attached to a belt around his waist, and the flat, dull noise it made contrasted with the jingles' sleigh-bell sounds. As the line of *Gah'e* moved close to the east-facing portion of the fire, they raised their black staffs and "cooed" the spirit sound. Backing away from the furious flames, they shuffled to the south and danced toward the burning wood again. Four times they blessed the fire; four times they prayed. While the *Gah'e* danced, Apache male singers and drummers walked across the arena carrying homemade drums. Sitting on a bench facing the east, the men balanced their small cylinders on their left thighs and began to pound the hide or rubber covers stretched over the open tops of the drums. In their right hands they held reeds or thick willow branches formed into circles at one end. These were the drumsticks. The sounds emanating from these Indian drums were unlike any other. While Navajo and Pueblo instruments have an internal echo, Apache drums emit a thick, solid, basso tympany, similar to the heavy male voices now beginning to sing after a medicine man's silent prayer.

Out of the darkness on the edge of the large circle a group of Apache women, most in their late twenties and early thirties, started to dance. They were joined shortly by an even younger coterie—girls in their middle to

Gah'e: Mountain Spirit dancers.
(Courtesy of Museum of New Mexico, negative no. 57774)

late teens. After this line passed, Mrs. Cleghorn and Mrs. Kanseah nodded at each other and approached the dance grounds. I followed.

Kathleen Kanseah was the unquestioned leader of our line. Mrs. Cleghorn stepped aside respectfully and permitted her cousin easy access to the inner circle. With her left foot first, Kathleen Kanseah stepped into the music in the darkness. In just a few seconds, her strong face was illuminated only by the fire. Her eyes were half closed, her mouth and chin were firm, her shoulders swung left and right, and her legs and moving feet kept the rhythm of the drums. Her mouth trembled slightly, as if silent words of prayer were struggling to be heard.

Mildred Cleghorn was right behind her. Tall and straight as an arrow, she stared into the fire as she entered the inner circle. Her rimless eyeglasses slipped down on her nose, but she didn't bring her hands out from under the shawl to adjust them. It was doubtful that she was even aware of the slippage. Her eyes were wide, her head just a bit forward. With shoulders squared and turning side to side, she melded into Kathleen Kanseah's cadence. Then she closed the space between them. With their rhythm joined, the two women moved in tandem, their heads, hearts, and bodies one with the music and the voices.

I was poised to follow Mrs. Cleghorn. I pulled the shawl closer around my shoulders and shivered, even though it was an August summer night and the fire was blazing. Not wanting to get too close, I deliberately kept a short distance between Mrs. Cleghorn and myself. Looking down at my feet, now moving contrary to the drums' rhythm, I wondered how I could ever imitate the dance step that these women had known since childhood. But, taking a deep breath, I entered the circle with my left foot, imitating Mrs. Kanseah. Now in line not too far behind Mrs. Cleghorn, I tried to move my shoulders from left to right, left to right, left to right, as my feet took small, shuffling steps. It didn't work. I couldn't do both at once. The fringe on my shawl was swinging, but not together with the music and not in rhythm with the two Apache women in front of me. I forgot about my feet and waited a split second until the position of Mrs. Cleghorn's shoulders matched my own. Then I turned them as she turned hers and kept that beat for a few long seconds. Doing OK. Now, back to the feet.

In the darkness, I couldn't see Mrs. Cleghorn's steps, so I couldn't imitate her, but I lifted my left foot a little higher than my right, skip-shuffled the next beat, and started the same process all over again. At last it seemed to be working. Then I turned my face to the fire and to the *Gah'e* dancing close to the flames.

With every sound, with every beat, with every inflection from the male voices, the *Gah'e* moved individually. They turned their bodies, swung their staffs, and cooed the spirit sound from beneath their black masks. The masks' tall, thin crowns split the night sky, and as the dancers bent their heads forward, the crowns were like antlers charging up to the flames. Their bare chests, painted black, were hot, sweating. The painted stars on their bodies, white against the black, ran in driblets in the dancers' sweat. The lightning bolts painted on their arms flowed through their hands into the staffs they carried. Their jingles made sleigh-bell noises; the young clown's cowbell joined in the music. Most of all, though, the sound of deep male voices filled the night with chants and the drumbeats carried the sound across the countryside and up to the eagles.

I was beginning to perspire but didn't dare loosen the shawl because all the other women now dancing were as tightly wrapped as I was. The warmth from the fire filled my face; I felt my forehead dampen. The singing and drumming seemed endless. My legs hurt, all the way from my feet to my hips. I looked at Mrs. Cleghorn's face for a sign of her pain. There was none. Maybe after seventy years of dancing this step Mildred Cleghorn had developed a special set of leg muscles only for dancing with the *Gah'e*. I certainly didn't have them. Worried that I couldn't go on, I looked for a way to step out of the circle when, abruptly, the drumming, the singing, and the dancing stopped.

Nearer to the fire, the *Gah'e* skipped around, waved their staffs, and slapped their legs. Neither Mrs. Kanseah nor Mrs. Cleghorn spoke to me or to each other. I looked over my shoulder at the people sitting on their chairs and discovered I was standing directly across from Mrs. Hugar and her family. I smiled at her but she didn't respond. I probably did something wrong by acknowledging her because no one else did anything but stand silently and wait for the drumming and the singing to begin again.

After a very short delay the men's voices once more filled the darkness. The two Apache women in front of me quickly started to move, as did the several other short lines of women who had gradually joined the inner circle of women dancers. Once again, in the center of the arena, the *Gah'e* cooed and shuffled or stomped toward the fire. This time it was easier for me to move my shoulders and feet, I felt more confidence, I drew closer to Mrs. Cleghorn. Still tucked into my black shawl, I swung my shoulders from side to side and was surprised that they kept pace with my feet. I developed an awareness of my surroundings. The darkness took on obscure forms. The firelight cast long orange shadows that distorted the faces of the *Gah'e*, the women dancers, and the observers. Apache women dancing in other groups appeared to be hypnotized, mesmerized, caught up in the ceaseless pounding of the drums, in wave after wave of words sung by the men in the ancient language. As we danced past the singers who were pounding their instruments, I thought I heard each of their voices individually. I saw sweat running in rivulets off their foreheads. The medicine man, sitting in the center of the group on the bench, sang the loudest, and the others followed his lead. Deep in prayer, his eyes were closed. One or two of the younger singers stared at me. A few seconds later I realized I was the only white woman dancing.

Stepping beyond the singers, I was lost in the music, in the primal pounding of the drum, in the swing of my shoulders, in the shuffle of my feet. I stared past the *Gah'e* into the flames and watched a curl of smoke rise from the middle of the stack of burning wood, then disappear into the blackness. One or two *Gah'e* came close to me, raised their staffs near my face, cooed, and danced away. I thanked them. My head was hot, my eyes saw things in the flames, the muscles around my waist hurt because of the constant turning of my shoulders, my legs ached desperately. It didn't matter. Filled with the spirit of the *Gah'e*, I stomped my feet on the dirt, raised my head, and stared into the fire.

Several other women had joined Kathleen Kanseah's line, and as we neared the singers and drummers again, I was amazed that we had danced around the circle so quickly. Lifted by the experience and wanting more, I felt as if I could go on forever.

Something in the voices of the singers beckoned. I felt it more and more. Dancing in front of the Apache men, I wondered and worried about what was happening, and I lost the rhythm. My shoulders sagged, my feet stopped. Quickly I tried to regain the step, but I couldn't. I followed Mrs. Cleghorn by walking, not dancing. The men stared at me, even as they continued pounding the drums and singing. I tried harder but couldn't get back in time with the music. Suddenly, an Apache male singer's voice said, "That's all right, white woman. Don't worry. You're doing just fine." Whoever he was, I will be eternally grateful.

Instantly, I rejoined Mildred Cleghorn's rhythm, swung my shoulders in time with hers, followed her feet with mine. And I prayed. Just as she was doing, just as Kathleen Kanseah was doing, just as Elbys Hugar—dancing directly opposite us with her eyes closed—was doing, just as the Apache women in line behind me were doing, and just as generations of Apache women have done. At long last, I felt part of the ancient, sacred ceremony. At long last, I was truly dancing with the *Gah'e*.

Notes

Chapter 1. Not So Long Ago

1. Opler, *Myths and Tales*, p. 111.
2. Barrett, *Geronimo*, pp. 12, 13.
3. Opler, *Myths and Tales*, p. 15.
4. Ibid., p. 111.
5. Perrone et al., *Medicine Women*, pp. 9–10.
6. Barrett, *Geronimo*, pp. 59–64.
7. Ibid., pp. 59–64.
8. Bourke, "Notes on Apache Mythology," p. 14.
9. Debo, *Geronimo*, p. 47.

10. Ellis, "Recollections of an Interview with Cochise," p. 391.
11. Ball, *Indeh*, p. 23.
12. Baldwin, *The Apache Indians*, pp. 143, 150–51.
13. Hodge, "The Early Navajo and Apache," pp. 232–40. In this excellent article Hodge describes the creation of the Navajo Tribe by the gods from two ears of corn and the subsequent coming together of various diverse indigenous peoples who became known as Navajo. He speaks geographically

when he states that three Apache clans came from southern New Mexico to join the Navajo, and this statement should not be construed to mean that the Apache originated in the south. In his continuing description of the Apache, Hodge adds "that by the continued addition of small bands of foreign or kindred peoples during the succeeding few decades, in a manner similar to the various Navajo adoptions, their importance to surrounding tribes gradually increased with their numbers and their aggressiveness with both." The expanded clans broke away from the larger group and went on to grow in size and strength. After the middle of the seventeenth century, the Apache were a very strong and forceful presence in the Southwest.

14. Goodwin, "White Mountain Apache Religion," pp. 26–27.

15. Mails, *The People Called Apache*, p. 76.

16. Opler, *Myths and Tales*, p. 15.

17. Mails, *The People Called Apache*, p. 78.

18. "Mescalero Maidens," *The Ruidoso News*, June 30, 1989.

19. Hoijer, *Chiricahua and Mescalero Apache Texts*, pp. 48–52.

20. Mails, *The People Called Apache*, p. 76.

21. Basso, *The Cibecue Apaches*, p. 17.

22. Davis, "Apache Debs," pp. 10–11, 40.

23. Ibid., p. 10.

24. Nicholas, "Mescalero Apache Girls' Puberty Ceremony," pp. 194–204.

25. Sonnichsen, *The Mescalero Apaches*, p. 30.

26. Basso, "The Gift of Changing Woman," pp. 119–72; Mails, *The People Called Apache*, pp. 313–19.

27. Mails, ibid., p. 236.

28. Ibid., p. 84.

29. Schut, interview, March 21, 1989. My emphasis on the Reformed Church of America in this book should not be construed to mean that only this church influenced the Apache people. At Mescalero especially, Father Albert and St. Joseph's Mission had an enormous effect on generations of Apaches.

30. Basso, "The Gift of Changing Woman," pp. 160–66.

31. M. Darrow, interview, September 23, 1989. Mr. Darrow did not specifically identify the anthropologists who believe that Apache society, historically, was patriarchal. Many, perhaps most, anthropologists feel that the social structure was matriarchal.

32. Perrone et al., *Medicine Women*, pp. 179–82. Part 4 of this book contains a description of witchcraft and its relationship to illnesses among the three cultures of the Southwest—Native American, Hispanic, and Anglo. Traditional cures are also explained.

33. Basso, "The Gift of Changing Woman," pp. 119–72.

34. Basso, *Western Apache Raiding*, pp. 267–69.

35. Schut, interview, March 21, 1989.

36. Ibid.

37. Ball, *Indeh*, p. 14.

38. Schut, interview, March 21, 1989.

39. Basso, *Western Apache Raiding*, pp. 267–69.

40. Ibid., pp. 267–69.

41. Mails, *The People Called Apache*, pp. 225–26.

42. Cole, "An Ethnohistory," p. 123.

43. Bourke, "The Medicine Men of the Apaches," pp. 468–69.

44. Ibid., pp. 468–69.

45. Stockel, "Lozen," pp. 20–22; Ball, *Indeh*, p. 62; Ball, *In the Days*, p. 128; Buchanan, *Apache Women Warriors*, pp. 32–38; Perrone et al., *Medicine Women*, pp. 19–80. Tu Moonwalker, an Apache healer, is featured among the medicine women described; she is a well-known basket weaver.

46. Ball, *Indeh*, p. 13.

47. Ibid., p. 99.

48. Mails, *The People Called Apache*, pp. 225–26.

49. Basso, *Western Apache Raiding*, pp. 284–87.

50. Flannery, "The Position of Women," pp. 26–32.

51. Worcester, *The Apaches*, photo, p. 309.

52. Flannery, "The Position of Women," pp. 26–32.

53. Baldwin, *The Apache Indians*, p. 143.

54. Cremony, *Life among the Apaches*, p. 249.

55. Barrett, *Geronimo*, pp. 43–44.

56. Sweeney, "I Had Lost All," p. 36, reports the facts from the Mexican perspective and is the first to identify by name the Mexicans involved and to reconstruct that episode as completely as possible.

57. Ball, *Indeh*, pp. 45–46.

58. Ibid., p. 57.

59. Skinner, *The Apache Rock Crumbles*, p. 223.

60. Baldwin, *The Apache Indians*, p. 143.

61. Haley, *Apaches*, p. 122.

62. Ibid., p. 122.

63. Ibid., p. 123.

64. Mails, *The People Called Apache*, p. 56.

65. Ibid., p. 57.

66. Haley, *Apaches*, pp. 124, 125.

67. Barrett, *Geronimo*, p. 25.

68. Terrell, *Apache Chronicle*, p. 93.

69. Ibid., p. 61.

70. Stockel, "Lozen," pp. 20–22; Ball, *Indeh*, p. 62; Ball, *In the Days*, p. 128; Buchanan, *Apache Women Warriors*, pp. 32–38.

Chapter 2.
Apache Women Warriors

1. Thrapp, *The Conquest of Apacheria*, p. 201.

2. Cole, "An Ethnohistory," p. 61.

3. M. Darrow, interview, September 23, 1989.

4. Ball, interview, May 1982.

5. Ball, *In the Days*, pp. 58, 146, 151; Ball, *Indeh*, pp. 3, 8, 13, 67, 68, 71, 72, 131, 204–10; Buchanan, *Apache Women Warriors*, p. 26; Debo, *Geronimo*, pp. 106n, 249.

6. U.S. Senate, Exec. Doc. 117 (49-2), p. 26. Alternate spellings are: Naiche for Natchez, Ahnandia for Ahwandia, Tishnolthoz for Fishnolth-tonz, Kayitah for Keyehtah.

7. Ibid., p. 26.

8. Ball and Sanchez, "Legendary Apache Women," p. 11.

9. Ibid., pp. 11–12.

10. Hugar, interview, May 8, 1989.

11. Ball, *In the Days*, pp. 168–74.

12. Ibid., pp. 37–38.

13. Hugar, interview, May 8, 1989.

14. Ball, *Indeh*, p. 8.

15. Thrapp, *Victorio*, p. 374.

16. Ball, *In the Days*, p. 15.

17. Wellman, *Death in the Desert*, pp. 147, 149.

18. Opler, *An Apache Lifeway*, p. 94.

19. *Memorials and Affidavits*, p. 30.

20. Ball, *Indeh*, p. 104.

21. Cremony, *Life among the Apaches*, p. 243. Cremony, a cavalry officer, recorded that Lozen was probably the woman

who received particular honor from the other sex but her Apache name has escaped from my memory. She was renowned as one of the most dextrous horse thieves and horse breakers in the tribe and seldom permitted an expedition to go on a raid without her presence. The translation of her Apache title was "Dextrous Horse Thief."

22. Stockel, "Lozen," pp. 20–22.

23. Ball, *In the Days*, p. 117.

24. Turcheneske, "The Apache Prisoners," p. v.

25. Ball, *Indeh*, pp. 138–39.

26. Welsh, *The Apache Prisoners*, p. 14.

27. Turcheneske, "The Apache Prisoners," p. v.

28. U.S. Senate, Doc. 432 (62-2), p. 5.

29. Stockel, "Lozen," pp. 20–22.

Chapter 3.
Apache Women from Mescalero

1. "Mescalero Apache Tales," Menu.

2. Ibid.

3. Debo, *Geronimo*, pp. 448–49.

4. Lockwood, *The Apache Indians*, p. 338.

5. Turcheneske, "Disaster at White Tail," p. 113.

6. Ibid., p. 123.

7. Ibid., p. 125.

8. Ibid., p. 125.

9. Lockwood, *The Apache Indians*, pp. 338–39.

10. Schut, interview, March 21, 1989.

11. Hugar, telephone conversation, May 15, 1989. Erecting a monument to commemorate the experiences of the Chiricahua Apache people at White-tail is, in my opinion, a two-edged sword. While the acknowledgment is certainly appropriate, one wonders if the monument will encourage tourism and, if so, what its effect would be on the pristine environment. Apache people today are very protective of Whitetail, to the extent of giving incorrect directions or insisting that the tourist receive permission from the tribal chairman before attempting to drive the long road.

12. *Weekly Arizonian*, September 17, 1870.

13. Hugar, interviews, April–August 1989.

14. Tyler, "Cochise," p. 5.

15. Ibid., p. 6.

16. Ibid., pp. 7–9, 10.

17. Cole, "An Ethnohistory," p. 60.

18. Ibid., p. 60.

19. Goodwin, *Among the Western Apache*, pp. 42–46.

20. Gaines, "Modern Day Warrior," p. 69.

21. Mitchell, conversation, September 23, 1989.

22. Kanseah, conversation, August 8, 1989.

23. Kanseah, interview, August 28, 1989.

24. Kanseah, conversation, September 21, 1989.

25. *Records of Medical History*. Oklahoma Genealogical Society, June 1984. The Lawton Public Library has a good deal of information about Apache prisoners of war, but the main source for this material is the Fort Sill Museum.

26. Ibid., pp. 32, 33, 35.

27. Ibid., p. 33.

28. Ibid., p. 34.

29. Ibid., p. 51.

30. Kanseah, conversation, September 21, 1989.

31. Kanseah, interview, August 28, 1989.

32. Kanseah, conversation, November 6, 1989.

Chapter 4.
Apache Women from Oklahoma

1. Pamphlet, Anadarko Chamber of Commerce.

2. Newsletter, National Hall of Fame for Famous American Indians.

3. Pamphlet, Indian City, USA.

4. Pamphlet, Fort Sill Museum.

5. Cemetery marker, Apache cemetery, Fort Sill, Oklahoma.

6. Wratten, "A Short Biographical Sketch." For a longer history of George Wratten's career, see Albert E. Wratten, "George Wratten Friend of the Apaches," *Journal of Arizona History*, vol. 27, no. 1 (Spring 1986), pp. 91–124. Footnote on p. 91 states,

Albert E. Wratten (1906–1979) was born on the Apache Indian Reservation near Fort Sill, Oklahoma, the youngest of five children. He spent his active years with the U.S. Postal Service, but his absorbing interest was in the career of his father, George M. Wratten, who devoted thirty-eight of his forty-seven years to the Apaches as government scout and interpreter, superintendent on three reservations, and persistent defender of their rights and interests. He never asked for or received any official recognition, and his son hoped to bring him the appreciation he deserved by printing his life story. He put together a 700 page manuscript but never found a publisher.

Albert E. Wratten was a child of George M. Wratten's second marriage; he was half brother to Amy and Blossom Wratten.

7. Griswold, "The Fort Sill Apaches."

8. *Lawton Morning Press-Constitutional*, December 31, 1981. Ruey Darrow nursed her mother constantly during the last year of Blossom's life. "It almost killed Ruey," commented Mildred Cleghorn.

9. Ibid. For a thorough descriptive history of earlier Apache relations with the U.S. government, see Robert M. Utley, "A Clash of Cultures: Fort Bowie and the Chiricahua Apaches" (Washington, D.C.: Department of the Interior, National Park Service, Government Printing Office, 1977).

10. Haozous, interview with Pat O'Brien, p. 4.

11. Ibid., pp. 4–5.

12. Ibid., pp. 5–6.

13. Ibid., p. 2.

14. Ibid., p. 5.

15. Ibid., p. 11.

16. Ibid., pp. 11–12.

17. *Chronicles of Oklahoma*, p. 453.

18. Haozous, interview with O'Brien, pp. 3–4.

19. Ibid., pp. 12–13.

20. Ibid., pp. 15–16.

21. M. Darrow, interview, September 23, 1989.

22. Ibid.

23. Turcheneske, "The United States Congress," p. 199.

24. Ibid., p. 211.

25. Ibid., p. 221.

26. Cleghorn, interview with author, August 8, 1989.

27. Murphy, correspondence with author, October 1989.

28. *Albuquerque Journal*, May 24, 1983.

29. Perlman, "Allan Houser."

30. Pamphlet, Wheelwright Museum.

31. *Albuquerque Journal*, September 16, 1986.

32. *Albuquerque Journal*, November 21, 1988.

33. Ibid.

34. *Albuquerque Journal*, September 27, 1986.

35. Ibid.

36. Cleghorn, interview with author, August 8, 1989.

37. *Albuquerque Journal*, November 23, 1988.

38. R. Darrow, conversation, September 22, 1989.

39. M. Darrow, correspondence, November 9, 1989.

40. M. Darrow, interview, September 23, 1989.

41. R. Darrow, interview, November 12, 1989.

42. R. Darrow, conversation, October 28, 1989.

43. R. Darrow, interview, November 12, 1989.

44. M. Darrow, interview, September 23, 1989.

45. R. Darrow, interview, November 12, 1989.

46. R. Darrow, interview, October 27, 1989.

Chapter 5.
Ceremonies and Celebrations

1. Hugar, conversation, July 1, 1989.

2. Ibid., July 14, 1989. Ceremonies are held when a young boy is initially affiliated with the *Gah'e* as a clown, but these rituals are private. One usually attends by invitation only.

3. Hugar, conversation, August 19, 1989.

4. Breuninger, conversation, September 28, 1989.

Bibliography

BOOKS

Baldwin, Gordon C. *The Apache Indians: Raiders of the Southwest*. New York: Four Winds Press, 1978.

Ball, Eve. *Indeh: An Apache Odyssey*. Provo: Brigham Young University Press, 1980.

——. *In the Days of Victorio*. Tucson: University of Arizona Press, 1970.

Barrett, S. M. *Geronimo: His Own Story*. New York: Ballantine Books, 7th printing, 1977.

——., ed. *Geronimo's Story of His Life*. New York: Duffield and Company, 1907.

Basso, Keith H. *The Cibecue Apaches*. New York: Holt, Rinehart and Winston, 1970.

——, ed. *Western Apache Raiding and Warfare from the Notes of Grenville Goodwin*. Tucson: University of Arizona Press, 1971.

Buchanan, Kimberly Moore. *Apache Women Warriors*. El Paso: Texas Western Press, 1986.

Cremony, John C. *Life among the Apaches*. San Francisco: A. Roman and Company, 1868. Reprint. Glorieta, N.M.: Rio Grande Press, 1969.

Debo, Angie. *Geronimo: The Man, His Time, His Place*. Norman: University of Oklahoma Press, 1976.

Goodwin, Grenville. *Among the Western Apache: Letters from the Field*. Ed. Morris E. Opler. Tucson: University of Arizona Press, 1973.

Haley, James L. *Apaches: A History and Culture Portrait*. Garden City, N.Y.: Doubleday and Company, 1981.

Hoijer, Harry. *Chiricahua and Mescalero Apache Texts with Ethnological Notes by Morris E. Opler*. Chicago: University of Chicago Press, 1938.

Lockwood, Frank C. *The Apache Indians*. Lincoln and London: University of Nebraska Press, 1938.

Mails, Thomas E. *The People Called Apache*. Englewood Cliffs, N.J.: Prentice-Hall, 1974.

Opler, Morris E. *An Apache Lifeway*. Chicago: University of Chicago Press, 1941.

———. *Myths and Tales of the Chiricahua Apache Indians*. New York: Kraus Reprint Company, 1969.

Perrone, Bobette, H. Henrietta Stockel, and Victoria Krueger. *Medicine Women, Curanderas, and Women Doctors*. Norman: University of Oklahoma Press, 1989.

Simmons, Marc. *Ranchers, Ramblers, & Renegades: True Tales of Territorial New Mexico*. Santa Fe: Ancient City Press, 1984.

Skinner, Woodward B. *The Apache Rock Crumbles: The Captivity of Geronimo's People*. Pensacola: Skinner Publications, 1987.

Sonnichsen, C. L. *The Mescalero Apaches*. 2d ed. Norman: University of Oklahoma Press, 1973.

Terrell, John Upton. *Apache Chronicle*. New York: World Publishing Company, 1972.

Thrapp, Dan L. *The Conquest of Apacheria*. Norman: University of Oklahoma Press, 1967.

———. *Victorio and the Mimbres Apaches*. Norman: University of Oklahoma Press, 1974.

Wellman, Paul I. *Death in the Desert*. New York: Pyramid Books, 1963.

Welsh, Herbert. *The Apache Prisoners in Fort Marion*. Philadelphia: Office of the Indian Rights Association, 1887.

Worcester, Donald E. *The Apaches: Eagles of the Southwest*. Norman: University of Oklahoma Press, 1979.

ARTICLES

Ball, Eve, and Lynda A. Sanchez. "Legendary Apache Women." *Frontier Times* (October–November 1980): pp. 8–12.

Basso, Keith H. "The Gift of Changing Woman." Smithsonian Institution Anthropological Papers, no. 76. *Bureau of American Ethnology Bulletin* 196 (1966): pp. 119–73.

Bourke, John G. "The Medicine Men of the Apaches." Bureau of Ethnology, *Ninth Annual Report*, 1887–1888. Glorieta, N.M.: Rio Grande Press: pp. 443–603.

———. "Notes on Apache Mythology." *Journal of the American Folklore Society*, vol. 3 (April–June 1890): pp. 209–12.

Davis, Anne Pence. "Apache Debs." *New Mexico* (April 1937): pp. 10–11, 40.

Ellis, A. N. "Recollections of an Interview with Cochise." *Kansas State Historical Society Collections*, vol. 13 (1913–1914): pp. 387–92.

Flannery, Regina. "The Position of Women among the Mescalero Apaches." *Primitive Man*, vol. 5 (April–July 1932): pp. 26–32.

Gaines, Judy. "Modern Day Warrior Champions Dignity for Mescalero Apaches." *New Mexico Magazine* (August 1989): pp. 67–76.

Goodwin, Grenville. "White Mountain Apache Religion." *American Anthropologist*, vol. 40: pp. 24–37. (1938).

Hodge, Frederick Webb. "The Early Navajo and Apache." *American Anthropologist*, vol. 8 (July 1895): pp. 232–40.

Nicholas, Dan. "Mescalero Apache Girls' Puberty Ceremony." *El Palacio*, vol. 46, no. 9 (September 1939): pp. 193–204.

Notes and Documents. *Chronicles of Oklahoma*, vol. 41 (Winter 1963–1964): pp. 450–62.

Perlman, Barbara. "Allan Houser: Songs from the Earth." *Southwest Art* (June 1981).

Sonnichsen, C. L. "The Remodeling of Geronimo." *Arizona Highways* (September 1986): pp. 2–11.

Stockel, H. Henrietta. "Lozen: Apache Warrior Queen." *Real West Magazine* (December 1982): pp. 20–22.

Sweeney, Edwin R. " 'I Had Lost All': Geronimo and the Carrasco Massacre of 1851." *Journal of Arizona History*, vol. 27, no. 1 (Spring 1986): pp. 35–52.

Turcheneske, John Anthony, Jr. "The United States Congress and the Release of the Apache Prisoners of War at Fort Sill." *Chronicles of Oklahoma*, vol. 54 (Summer 1976): pp. 199–226.

———. "Disaster at White Tail: The Fort Sill Apaches' First Ten Years at Mescalero, 1913–1923." *New Mexico Historical Review*, vol. 53, no. 2 (April 1978): pp. 109–132.

Tyler, Barbara. "Cochise: Apache War Leader, 1858–1861." *Journal of Arizona History*, vol. 6 (1965): pp. 1–10.

NEWSPAPERS

Albuquerque Journal, May 24, 1983; September 16, 1986; September 27, 1986;
    November 21, 1988; November 23, 1988.
Arizona Citizen, April 15, 1876.
Lawton Morning Press-Constitutional, December 31, 1981.
The Ruidoso News, June 30, 1989.
Weekly Arizonian, September 17, 1870.

DISSERTATIONS

Cole, Donald C. "An Ethnohistory of the Chiricahua Indian Reservation, 1872–
    1876." Ph.D. diss., University of New Mexico, 1981.
Turcheneske, John Anthony, Jr. "The Apache Prisoners of War at Fort Sill, 1894–
    1914." Ph.D. diss., University of New Mexico, 1978.

GOVERNMENT PUBLICATIONS

Memorials and Affidavits Showing Outrages Perpetuated by the Apache Indians in
    the Territory of Arizona for the Years 1869 and 1870. San Francisco: Francis and
    Valentine, Printers, 1871.
Twelfth Census of the United States. Indian Population, Oklahoma Territory,
    June 1, 1900.
U.S. Senate Executive Document 117, vol. 2449, 49th Cong., 2d sess.
U.S. Senate Document 432, vol. 6175, 62d Cong., 2d sess.

MISCELLANEOUS PUBLICATIONS

Menu. Geronimo's Southwest Deli at the Top O' The Inn.
Newsletter. National Hall of Fame for Famous American Indians.
Pamphlet. Anadarko Chamber of Commerce.
Pamphlet. Fort Sill Museum.
Pamphlet. Indian City, USA.
Pamphlet. Wheelwright Museum.
Records of Medical History of Fort Sill, Indian Territory, February 1873–May 1880, and
    of Fort Sill, Oklahoma, 1903–1913. Extracted and indexed by Polly Lewis Murphy.
    (Southwest Oklahoma Genealogical Society, Lawton, Oklahoma, June 1984).

UNPUBLISHED MATERIAL

Griswold, Gillett. "The Fort Sill Apaches: Their Vital Statistics, Tribal Origins, Antecedents." U.S. Army Artillery and Missile Center Museum Archives, Fort Sill, Oklahoma.
Wratten, Albert E. "A Short Biographical Sketch of the Life of George M. Wratten, Government Scout and Interpreter for the Apache Prisoners of War."

INTERVIEWS, CONVERSATIONS, AND CORRESPONDENCE

Ball, Eve. Interview with author. May 1982.
Breuninger, Evelyn. Conversation with author. September 28, 1989.
Cleghorn, Mildred I. Interview with author. August 8, 1989.
Darrow, Michael. Interview with author. September 23, 1989. Correspondence with author. November 9, 1989.
Darrow, Ruey. Interviews and conversations with author. September 22, October 27–29, November 12, 1989.
Haozous, Blossom W. Interview with Pat O'Brien. July 22, 1976. Bicentennial Oral History Program for the U.S. Army Field Artillery and Fort Sill Museum. Fort Sill, Oklahoma.
Hugar, Elbys. Interviews and conversations with author. March 21, April 7, May 8, May 15, June 9, July 1, July 14, August 19, 1989.
Kanseah, Kathleen. Interview and conversations with author. August 28, September 21, November 6, 1989.
Mitchell, Roy (son of Watson Mithlo, Apache prisoner of war). Conversation with author. September 23, 1989.
Murphy, Polly Lewis. Correspondence with author. October 1989.
Schut, Rev. Robert. Interview with author. March 21, 1989.

MISCELLANEOUS

Cemetery Marker. Apache Cemetery, Fort Sill, Oklahoma.

Index

Page numbers for photographs are indicated by italic type.

Housing, 125, 156; at Whitetail, 56–57, 58–59, 61–62, 78; in Oklahoma, 113, 115; traditional, *13*, *23*, *73*
Huera, *66*
Hugar, Charles, 78–79, 86
Hugar, Elbys Naiche, xxiv–xxv, 60, 63–87, *64*, 103, 159; childhood memories of, xxiii, 34–35, 37–38, 69, 72–78; at *Gah'e* ceremony, 174, 178
Hunting, 14, 15

Illness, 11, 49–50, 51, 73, 76, 93
Imach, Mildred, 109, *110*
Imach, Myrtle, 109, *110*
Imach, Richard (Ee-nah), xxiii, 109
Imprisonment, xxii, 7, 39, *44*, *50*, 74–75, 133; conditions during, 49–50, 65, 91; death during, xxiv, 16–17, 91–93; of Geronimo, 7, 23, 31–32, 128; release from, 51, 106, 122–124, 130, 144
In the Days of Victorio (Kaywaykla and Ball), 39
Indian baseball, 74
Indian City, USA, 104, 174
Indian Organization Act, 55
Indian Princess, 102, 152, 161, 173
Indian Rights Association, 122
Infanticide, 26
Infants, 9, *21*, 26, 27
Ishton, xxiv, 16, 39, 41, 111

Jeffries, Clarence R., 57
Juh, Chief, 16, 39, 41

Kanseah, Jasper, 89
Kanseah, Kathleen Smith, xxiii, 88–99, *90*, 131, 170; and cultural preservation, xxv, 153; at *Gah'e* ritual, 173, 174–176
Kanseah, Lee, 89
Kaydoso, Pamela, 161, 167
Kaywaykla, 39, 40
Kaywaykla, James, 37, 39, 48
Kenoi, Katherine, 136, 166

Killer of Enemies, 8–9
Kiowa Tribe, 51, 102
Klah, Hosteen, 103
Kuni. *See* Coonie

Land allotment, 51, 122–124, 125
Language, 80–82; preservation of, 84, 85, 120, 142, 153–154, 165–166
Laundry, 78
Leadership, 12, 23
Legends, 1–4, 5–6, 25, 47–48
Legends. *See also* Creation myths
Light, William A., 57–58
Lipan Apache Tribe, 54–55
Little, Martina, 89
Livestock, 57, 58, 59, 74–75
Lozen, xxiv, 47–48, 184n.21; imprisonment of, 32, *44*, 51; as medicine woman, 16, 28, 41–42; surrender of, 31, 43, 49; as warrior, 28, 29–30, 43, 46

Magoosh-Shanta, Ceda, 161
Mails, Thomas, 6–7, 9–10, 17, 26
Marianetta, *129*
Marriage, 4–5, 19, 22–25, 47, 78, 93, 132
Massasoit, 103
Matriarchal society, 10, 12, 17, 182n.31
Medicine, 23, 76, 81, 171
Medicine men, 6, 9, 16, 25, 27, 179
Medicine tepee, 158
Medicine women, 15–16, 19, 25, 27, 28, 41–42, 48, 183n.45
Mescalero Apache Cultural Center, 63, 68, 73, 167–168
Mescalero Apache Dictionary (Breuninger and Hugar), 81–82, 165
Mescalero Apache Reservation, 53–55. *See also* Whitetail
Mescalero Apache Tribe, 53–99; formation of, 54–55; heritage day, 164–168; puberty ceremony, 7–9, 155–164
Mescalero Reformed Church. *See* Reformed churches